Dare to Rejoice

CARDINAL JEAN-MARIE LUSTIGER

Compiled and introduced by Edward Wakin, Ph.D.

Dare to Rejoice

A Celebration of Christian Life

Our Sunday Visitor Publishing Division
Our Sunday Visitor, Inc.
Huntington, Indiana 46750

Copyright © 1990
by Our Sunday Visitor Publishing Division
Our Sunday Visitor, Inc.
ALL RIGHTS RESERVED

Our Sunday Visitor Publishing Division
Our Sunday Visitor, Inc.
200 Noll Plaza
Huntington, Indiana 46750

International Standard Book Number: 0-87973-436-1
Library of Congress Catalog Card Number: 89-62938

*Cover design by Rodney Needler; photograph by Anita Nicholas
Back-cover illustration by Monica Watts*

Published in the United States of America
436

TABLE OF CONTENTS

The Sounds of Faith

The words of Cardinal Jean-Marie Lustiger are the sounds of faith.

It is the faith of a pastoral cardinal who confronts both believer and nonbeliever with reminders that the problems of the modern world are fundamentally spiritual.

It is the faith of a committed churchman who has little patience with the lukewarm, on-the-other-hand, get-along Christian.

It is the faith of a sophisticated intellectual devoted to simple prayer and uncomplicated devotion.

It is the faith of a teenage convert from Judaism who, when asked about his "discovery" of Christianity, answers: "It was as though I knew about it already. I do not mean customs, rites, practices, but the content of Christianity. I seemed to have known it beforehand."

It is the faith of a man still "surprised" by Christians who don't understand their faith: "Those affirmations that touch on the mystery of God, the meaning of revelation through Christ, God's call to humanity — to His people — are evident to me. They are a part of the logic of faith, and I am stupefied to discover that there are believers, steeped in Christianity since childhood, who do not understand this."

It is the faith of someone who discovered Christianity and has a gift for helping others grasp the joy of believing in Christ.

In print, in the pulpit, in person-to-person encounters, the words of the cardinal-convert leave an imprint on the faithful, the doubting, and the disaffected. No encounter with him and his strong personality is casual. Intense, focused, forceful, he gets to his point directly. He makes his feelings as well as his meaning clear. His eloquence in French carries over into his workable English. The jutting of his chin, the furrowing of his brow, the determined look alternating with a slightly mischievous smile provide visual cues for words that attack a subject head-on, whether he's agreeing or disagreeing, challenging or seconding. He exhilarates.

Cardinal Lustiger is a graceful warrior for his faith but not a special pleader. He demonstrates no need to play rhetorical games or to make emotional sales pitches for the messages imbedded in his faith. As he says, he's "surprised" when others who should know better miss his fundamental point of departure, which is faith in the Messiah.

Simply put in his own words, "Christianity concerns the whole of life" and the role of today's Christians is to be "the witnesses of the transcendent role of man." For him, "If you believe in the Gospel, then you believe in the Church. . . . If you believe in the Gospel, then you see the Church as the sacrament of a world renewed and the anticipation of a new humanity."

He doesn't sell the Christian message in the style of a TV evangelist or trumpet its blessings like a religious salesman. He asserts it, never doubting that it's what humanity needs in order to fulfill itself and for the world to survive. He mixes the biblical fire and brimstone of the Old Testament with the loving concern of the New Testament. A man of righteous anger . . . a look of wrath that thunders wordlessly. A man of personal warmth . . . an outburst of contagious laughter. A "living provocation," as he aptly describes himself. Appropriately, he titled two celebrated collections of his sermons, talks, articles, and interviews *Dare to Believe* and *Dare to Live*.

The many faces he shows in photographs do him justice. The intense, dark eyes mirror his moods, alternately pensive, reflective, outgoing, argumentative, attentive, prayerful, absorbed, annoyed, concerned, responsive. Amid the changing messages in the eyes, his granite chin holds firm with a continuing statement of strength and determination. Face to face, he recalls Father Hesburgh of Notre Dame with an outgoing, no-nonsense style of dealing with people whose job is asking questions. Both men send a similar unspoken message: *I'm happy to answer your questions. But don't waste my time. Get to the point. And don't be offended if I let you know that I dismiss the implications or assumptions of a question.*

Two informed witnesses to the blend of Lustiger faith and persona are a non-practicing Jew, Jean-Louis Missika, and a doubting Catholic, Dominique Wolton. (Of themselves, they say, "One doesn't believe; the other can't be certain.") They spent five months probing, examining, questioning, and dialoguing with Cardinal Lustiger to produce a transcript of 1,800 pages. The result was a publishing phenomenon. The cardinal's words, in a book titled *The Choice of God*, flew in the face of the anti-clerical, secular world of Paris intellectuals to become a No. 1 nonfiction best seller in France. Interlocutors Missika and Wolton captured the essence of the cardinal's message, its relevance, and its impact:

"He is trying to think through his faith without either opposing reason or submitting to it. He rejects the temptation of going along with the social and political values of our time, but he also rejects the retreat of religion into private life. He is neither traditionalist nor modernist, because he simply does not think of religion in those terms."

Faith dictates the way the cardinal thinks of religion, not the politics of the day, not the arguments between factions, not the jockeying for position of power groups, not the collision between social classes, not the struggle for dominance. Clearly, once converted, he accepted fully — his Jewish heritage and his Catholic commitment. The result is a man of clarity, conviction, and conscience. Also a complicated man.

The cardinal has the clear vision of the outsider who often sees what those growing up inside the faith have overlooked. His journey to Baptism and Holy Orders meant discovering what was there in the Messiah for him as a Jewish boy named Aron and what was there in the Catholic Church for him as a priest. He grew up Jewish in Paris, the son of a dry goods store owner who spoke of persecution and pogroms in his native Poland. An outsider as a Jewish child in Catholic Paris, he became an outsider at home, secretly reading the New Testament. He became "particularly impressed" by the continuity between the Old and New Testament and in his teens came the decision to convert to Catholicism.

He recalls as "perfectly unbearable" the scene in which he informed his parents of his decision. He had to tell parents whom he revered and who had "warned" him about Christians. Even "the good ones can become bad, and then, they kill." The 14-year-old of that parental confrontation fathered a churchman ready for confronting a secular world with the force of his faith.

After the Nazis occupied Paris in World War II, he went to live with a Catholic family in Orléans, where he was baptized (also the city where he returned as bishop in 1979). His parents stayed behind in Paris, his father in hiding, his mother running the family dry-goods store in the Montparnasse section of Paris. On September 10, 1942, his mother was arrested and sent to Auschwitz, where she perished in that dread extermination camp. When her teenage son learned of her death, he exclaimed in anguish, "I'll never again be able to laugh."

At 21, he once again challenged family sensibilities and experienced a "very cruel, very brutal conflict" with his father who had survived the war. He had decided to respond to the "Call of God" and in 1946 told his father of the decision to enter the seminary. It took two years to heal the wound and bring about a reconciliation, a time when father and son did not see each other. By the time the elder Lustiger died at age 82, his determined son, Aron, was archbishop of Paris, a cardinal, and "*papabile*" — a possibility for the papacy. (The cardinal selected Jean-Marie at baptism as names with both Jewish and Christian origins.)

After ordination, he was appointed chaplain at the Sorbonne, a challenging assignment but one that was outside the normal path to higher positions in the French church. He didn't do graduate work in Rome and never worked in the formation of priests. He spent fifteen years (1954 to 1969) as a chaplain outside the traditional clerical network for getting ahead.

Outside, but not obscure. In 1963, with a letter to Pope John XXIII, he arranged a spirited meeting between the Pope and a group of French students led by Chaplain Lustiger. The visitors made a strong impression upon the Pope, so much so that a small Lustiger legend arose from the encounter. The dying Pontiff recalled the Lustiger students and asked about them on his deathbed.

In ten years (1969-1979) spent as pastor of Ste. Jeanne de Chantal, an active, well-to-do parish in Paris, the cardinal demonstrated the approach that has stamped his role as Archbishop of Paris. The liturgy was the focus of parish life and the pastor forceful in leading his parishioners. His magnetic sermons gained attention and attracted a publisher who brought out *Sermons of a Parish Priest of Paris*. A knowledgeable observer described the lasting Lustiger imprint evident in the words of the sermons: "emotional, intense, highly spiritual reflections."

A gift for public address and his personal magnetism caught the attention of the Apostolic Delegate, and overnight the convert from Judaism was thrust onto a larger stage. He was named bishop of the prestigious see of Orléans when it became unexpectedly vacant in 1979. Eighteen months later, he became archbishop of Paris. A surprising appointment to Orléans was followed by an amazing appointment to Paris, surprising and amazing for Lustiger and the French Church in general.

Almost immediately, observers pointed to a "Paris version of the Pope." Both charismatic, both articulate, both intellectuals who emphasize religious devotion, they are also outsiders — the Polish Pope in Rome, the Jewish-Polish cardinal in Paris. Each is modern and enlightened in style, while strongly committed to the traditions and orthodox doctrines of the Catholic Church. Not surprisingly, they have forged a close relationship sustained by regular Lustiger visits to Rome.

From his appointment in 1981, the new archbishop of Paris attracted worldwide attention as an unexpected choice with an unusual background. He neither sought nor evaded confrontation as he asserted his presence. After his appointment, I watched him in his first meeting with a horde of 80 French journalists, moving freely among them and then responding to their bombardment of questions with direct, lively, forthright answers. He wore a black velour corduroy suit and Roman collar, visually announcing his freedom from pomp and circumstance. His manner and mode of answering questions announced that Paris had a candid new archbishop with commitment and determination.

I met him privately for the first time after that meeting and since then have stayed in direct touch with developments in the French church during repeated visits to France. Late in the 1980s, the archbishop, now cardinal, was as forceful as ever during a personal meeting in which we discussed what had happened to him and to the Church. He spoke not of political or financial power, but of moral power. What counted for him was not strategy, but "the question of faith — faith and prayer." His message had not changed.

The same message, but now a churchman with an international following. The former chaplain and pastor of a Paris church has greatly expanded the audience for the distinctive Lustiger brand of faith, inspiration, and proclamation of Christianity. He has traveled abroad, including the United States. His sermons, lectures, articles, and books have been published in several languages. He has become a forceful spokesman for the faith he discovered as a boy and is in demand for a wide range of observations, commentary, and inspiring reflections.

This collection seeks to do justice to the many sides of his basic message of faith. The words that follow were chosen to reflect the force of the convert-cardinal and the variety of ways he expresses his views to believers and nonbelievers. The cardinal does not talk to make conversation nor set down words to fill empty spaces, but to celebrate faith and its contagious joy for those who have its gift. Anyone who pays attention is bound to feel the impact.

The resistant agnostic, Dominique Wolton, who engaged the cardinal in lengthy dialogue, admits that after close contact with this man of faith, he was changed. That contact "accentuated the importance of the spiritual question in my daily, intellectual, and political life."

For believers, the Lustiger words of faith have far greater effect. His words celebrate a faith that a long-ago convert exemplifies and proclaims. Believers will find an affirmation of lived faith which rediscovers Christian joy amid joyless materialism. The result is inevitable: spreading the message of Christianity.

How to 'Listen' to This Book

The Word of God is the spoken word — from the Sermon on the Mount to the Sunday sermon from the pulpit — and those who speak that Word belong to the noble profession of preaching.

It is not the pulpit that makes the preacher; it's speaking the Word in person to others — to a congregation, to an interviewer, to a radio or TV audience. It's a fundamental commitment of Cardinal Lustiger. "I want to be able to preach freely," he told me shortly after his appointment as archbishop of Paris. He has done exactly that during the 1980s, making possible this rich and relevatory harvest of his preaching in sermons and interviews.

Because these were spoken words in the first place, the reader is "listening" in tranquillity to what was said, able to savor both the manner and substance. Withal, the words have the force and naturalness of speech without in any way sacrificing substance to verbal style.

These selections present the witness of a religious leader who has been described as one of the leading spiritual figures of our day. He represents preaching at its highest level: those who preach, not because they have to, but because they have something to say.

The cardinal's message for our times is unequivocal throughout its ramifications:

The crisis of today is spiritual.

So its solution must be spiritual.

He never lets his audience — whether it's one or many, humble or high-born, skeptic or believer — forget that beginning and end of what he says about Christian faith in today's world.

Because preaching is a personal act, the preacher's impact is tied to the indefinable, but undeniable, quality of presence. The word itself — *presence* — has a distinctly French ring, embodying the full force of an individual's personality and strength of character. Presence is projected by the individual in person — by the sound of voice, by gestures and facial expressions, by turns of phrase and favorite words.

Imagine the sound of the cardinal's firm, lively voice as you read these once-spoken, now-read words. The voice vibrates with life, varying within a modest range as it registers the solemn, the serious, the assertive, the humane sides of the preacher.

Picture the panorama of changing expressions of a preacher absorbed in what he's saying, registering the feelings that parallel the meaning of the words.

Hear clear, strong, resonant French gliding through sentences with strong endings and thoughtful pauses.

Most of all, remember that these are words of conviction forged in study and thought, developed with intellectual vigor, and infused with powerful faith.

Read, then, and "listen" carefully for preaching of the Word of God.

Part I

REJOICE
IN THE LORD

After his appointment as Archbishop of Paris in February 1981, Cardinal Lustiger addressed a letter to the Christians of Paris. He began by asking himself the question, "What word does God desire that I tell you?"

His answer for himself and for the Christians of Paris was "You are loved. Yes, God loves you."

He called it "my first word."

It is his continuing word, as is evident in this section, "Rejoice in the Lord," a selection of his sermons in the years since his appointment.

Blessed Hope *

In "Blessed Hope," Cardinal Lustiger leads Christians through life in a panoramic, faith-filled view of the journey. A dedicated, personal, and relevant guide, he always keeps the Lord in sight as the guide of guides, the source of strength for the strong, the goal of the goal-seeker.

In eleven sermons — delivered over Radio Notre- Dame in Paris from April 20 to June 29, 1988 — the impact of his theme is cumulative, the distinctive benefit of reading the sermons continuously rather than hearing them on successive Wednesdays in Paris. Note also the seamless fabric of his preaching: the phrase, "blessed hope," caps an earlier series of sermons, "You Shall Love the Lord Your God," delivered almost three years previously.

Along the way, you can stop to register his memorable phrases: "the world's ephemeral beauty," its "precarious splendor," "the fleeting glimmer of the good in history."

In particular, you can reflect on his affirmations. In baptism, the infant's future is "astonishingly visible: he has become a child of God, he shares the dignity of Christ — priest, prophet, and king — and he is a Temple of the Holy Spirit. . . ." "In the Eucharist, we experience the conclusion of the journey while we are still on the road. How powerful our hope is!. . . ." Christian hope gives the couple joined in matrimony "a superhuman strength for their daily life, and allows them to go forward with a perspective which surpasses our earthly horizon."

At the end of this series of sermons there is ringing affirmation of the "secret beauty" of every life: "It is the love that God has for you. Yes, for you — just as you are. By the sacrament of mercy, this love is progressively revealed to us throughout our lives."

---

*Sermons translated by Rebecca H. Balinski.

I

'Do Not Be Anxious. . . .'

What exactly is Christian hope?

It is our resurrection in the resurrected Christ!

In St. Paul's vivid phrase (Ti 2:13), it is our "blessed hope." We recall it at every Mass with the words inserted in the Lord's Prayer during the fifth century when the Church was a victim of barbarian invasions: "In your mercy keep us free from sin and protect us from all anxiety as we wait in joyful hope for the coming of our Savior, Jesus Christ." In other words, as we await our resurrection, our "blessed hope."

In everyday language, the word "hope" is ambigious. It can mean a positive way of looking at the future—optimistically, with dreams of a better tomorrow—and can have all sorts of worldly objectives such as exotic vacations, health, success, "happiness." In short, hope can appear to belong to an imaginary realm, to depend on changing emotions and moods, to be directed toward a more less undetermined future. What does this kind of hope have to do with Christian hope? How can Christian hope influence our daily behavior?

To answer these questions I remind you of the singular definition of faith which is at the same time a definition of hope found in the Epistle to the Hebrews (11:1): "Now faith is the assurance of things hoped for, the conviction of things not seen." Faith is the substance of things hoped for, and hope is the object of faith.

Faith and hope are so closely linked that what is hoped for through faith is not just anything! Faith concerns our salvation, that is, our union with Christ, Son of God, in such a way that through him, with him, in him — having been sanctified and having become children of God — we are resurrected in our turn. Faith allows us to reach,

17

in the present, the reality we are hoping for. It allows us to share already in Christ's Resurrection through which our existence, like that of all humanity, is transfigured.

Since hope is fundamentally linked to the mystery of the resurrected Christ and to our own resurrection, you have possibly concluded that this theological virtue is very difficult to live up to. Péguy called it *"petite espérance"* when he sang about it in Le Porche: "It is too often forgotten that of the three theological virtues, it is definitely the most difficult, and is surely the one most pleasing to God. The faith I like best, God says, is hope."

Then how is it possible to live in hope?

We can assess what such an attitude implies from Jesus' words: "Therefore I tell you, do not be anxious about your life, what you shall eat or what you shall drink, nor about your body, what you shall put on. Is not life more than food, and the body more than clothing? Look at the birds of the air: they neither sow nor reap nor gather into barns, and yet your heavenly Father feeds them. Are you not of more value than they? And which of you being anxious can add one cubit to his span of life? And why are you anxious about clothing? Consider the lilies of the field, how they grow; they neither toil nor spin; yet I tell you, even Solomon in all his glory was not arrayed like one of these. But if God so clothes the grass of the field, which today is alive and tomorrow is thrown into the oven, will he not much more clothe you, O men of little faith? Therefore do not be anxious, saying, 'What shall we eat?' or 'What shall we drink?' or 'What shall we wear?' For the Gentiles seek all these things; and your heavenly Father knows that you need them all. But seek first his kingdom and his righteousness, and all these things shall be yours as well. Therefore do not be anxious about tomorrow, for tomorrow will be anxious for itself. Let one day's own trouble be sufficient for the day" (Mt 6:25-34).

Does not Jesus' insistent counsel against anxiety, like His brusque condemnation of the "insane" rich man who has stored up his grain in barns (Lk 12:16-21), simply encourage a lack of foresight, a kind of happy go-lucky lifestyle which is in contradiction with "blessed hope"?

Does it not foster the kind of heedlessness shown by the grasshopper in the fable — indeed, the kind of recklessness of which youth is so often accused?

No, on the contrary, by His advice Jesus is proposing an act of faith which is rooted in hope.

Living in the present by overcoming all cares, anxiety, and fears means hoping in God more than we are despairing in ourselves or are afraid for ourselves.

Living from day to day does not mean that we have nothing to worry about. It means entrusting ourselves to God, not with the illusion that God is going to solve all our problems or compensate for our irresponsibility, but with faith that the contradictions of existence are as nothing alongside this fundamental certitude: our lives are in God's hands, and God wants to give us His life, eternal life, through our communion with His love and by the power of the resurrected Christ.

Unless a person is completely unconscious, it is impossible to live in tranquillity day after day, surmounting the dread of what tomorrow may bring, without the assurance of God's love as described by the Apostle Paul: "We know that in everything God works for good with those who love him, who are called according to his purpose. . . . For I am sure that neither death, nor life, nor angels, nor principalities, nor things present, nor things to come, nor powers, nor height, nor depth, nor anything else in all creation, will be able to separate us from the love of God in Christ Jesus our Lord" (Rom 8:28, 38-39).

Yes, as Péguy writes, we must show our confidence in God by having hope in him.

II

With God, All Things Are Possible

Have you ever stopped to think about what every Christian can and ought to hope for?

To become a saint!

Of course, you are skeptical because you know yourself all too well. Furthermore, you may point out that there are even passages in the Gospel which seem to discourage such a thought. For example, when Jesus says: "You will know them by their fruits. Are grapes gathered from thorns, or figs from thistles? So, every sound tree bears good fruit, but the bad tree bears evil fruit" (Mt 7:16-17). From that you have deduced that "the die is cast": there are sound trees — all those canonized and uncanonized saints — and there is the multitude of all the others who can only be the "bad trees."

"What can anybody do about it," you say. "Heredity, education and all sorts of other factors 'determine' our destiny. Becoming a saint is no more the object of our hope than of our desire. The die is cast!"

Of course, you know your limitations, your temperament, your faults. So you have resigned yourself: "My character is like that. I cannot change it. I am not a saint and never will be!"

But just what is your idea of saintliness?

Is it really a matter of changing yourself to reach an ideal you may have dreamt about? Just as if you decide to lose six pounds or get yourself "into shape"? Is it a matter of changing your appearance, your "look"? Or does it have to do with responding to what God calls you to do? Of doing what He asks of you?

If God asks you to change a character trait, to go against your basic nature — even though it may seem impossible from a human point of view — you should hope to be able to make that change: "For with God nothing will be impossible" (Lk 1:37). The hope that the One who resurrected Christ can accomplish in you what He asks, ought to give you the strength to undertake the task, for love of God and your neighbor.

But if God does not ask it of you, then hope that He will give you the grace to adapt yourself — patiently and humbly — to your failings and your temperament, and that He will teach you not to make others suffer too much from them.

However, there is a secret despair which is more difficult to bear spiritually: since God's light makes it possible for us to discover our sin and how contrary it is to God's love, we may forever wish to change our lives while over and over again we are brought face to face with our weaknesses. In spite of our resolutions, the same old refusals, the same sidestepping, the same sins force us to recognize the "hopeless" gap between the "hope" of a flawless love and our inability to change ourselves and become saints.

Again I ask: just what is your idea of saintliness?

Is it not, in the first place, the condition of being saved when we were lost?

Otherwise, what is Christian hope? He who resurrected Christ from the dead lets us share in that Resurrection *now*, and makes us "saints" by continually snatching us from the jaws of death which is created by sin.

God's forgiveness is incessantly resurrecting us, lifting us up when we are sinking or losing our footing. Remember Peter's walk on the water (Mt 14:30ff)? God's forgiveness is not simply a matter of setting the meter back to zero, or an easygoing or humbling leniency. In the course of our spiritual combat for a life with Christ, it is a re-creation, a resurrection.

Never let yourself be buried by the shame of your sin, by the humiliation of discovering yourself to be so vulnerable, by the despair of a wounded pride. Humbly facing the all powerful divine forgiveness, have hope in God's mercy. Even though your heart condemns you, remember that God is greater than our hearts (cf. 1 Jn 3:20).

It is the resurrected Christ who restores you to life. It is He who gives you the hope of holiness. Rather than being overwhelmed and discouraged by your sins, be thankful for the forgiveness which is repeatedly offered and, if you desire it, repeatedly received.

The hope of becoming a saint means trusting in God, not in ourselves. It means believing that whatever God asks of us, he makes it possible for us to accomplish.

III

When Love Fails. . . .

What meaning does Christian hope have when there is a rupture in marital fidelity, when parental love is rebuffed, when death strikes? In a word, what meaning can it have in face of any heartbreaking event which seems to be irremediable?

When a marriage breaks up, regardless of its duration and mutual fidelity, the Christian plan which sealed the union of a man and a woman can appear to be an illusion or an absurdity. When love has died, what remains to be hoped for?

And what can be said to comfort parents whom their children have rejected? Years may go by without renewed relations. What can they still hope for?

Even more cruel is death, which ends all hope of restored communication since it permanently seals the absence. How can wrongs be righted, injuries be forgiven? How can relations be resumed? What is to be done about the regret, sometimes the deep remorse, over something that was done or not done? Certainly, we repent. But is it possible to hope for a reconciliation?

Are these three situations then examples of hopeless failures? No, but the specifically Christian response to them, far from soothing us with illusions, requires a labor of faith — that is, an act of hope whose demands are painful.

In fact, these lost fidelities, these broken relations, these presences snatched away from us, force us to bring up the question of forgiveness. To the wounded party, it can seem impossible. Does God really demand it? How far do we have to go?

For the Christian, forgiveness is above all the experience of his or her own forgiveness received from God. In the Sacrament of Penance, we are given the grace to be able to confess our sins and to ask to be ''delivered'' from them. How prodigious God's mercy is! It is not just something to relieve our guilt, or erase the past; nor can it be compared to a reduced sentence or an amnesty. Forgiveness received from God is a resurrection from the dead. Sin literally kills us, crushes and annihilates us. Through the gift of the Spirit, the heavenly Father's pardon reestablishes us in our integrity, restores us to life, puts us back on our feet alongside Christ, conqueror of death.

From the moment that God forgives us, we can and must hope to forgive each other so that love can be reborn.

The ruptures mentioned earlier are so profound that they appear to be irreparable. However by the grace received from the Sacrament of Penance, we already share in the experience of God's forgiveness. This experience lets us glimpse what lies beyond, on the horizon of our earthly pilgrimage: once their lives are completed and they are "filled with all the fullness of God" (cf. Eph 3:19), men and women whom sin and death have separated, will receive each other in the unique forgiveness received from God and mutually shared. Yes, enemies will embrace each other, fulfilling Isaiah's prophecy: "The wolf and the lamb shall feed together" (65:25).

That is our hope!

Illusory, you think? But our lives are not limited to what our senses lead us to understand, and they do not stop with death, which is only a necessary passage in our lives. Well beyond the ephemeral duration of biological existence, man receives from God, his Creator, the strength to endure for the "length of days for ever and ever" (Ps 21:4).

In communion with the resurrected Christ, we believe that our lives will be transfigured at our own resurrection. The graces given by God at this time in our lives are mere seeds which will bear their fruit for eternity. Our wounds and heartbreaks borne by Christ's Passion will be healed and metamorphosed, by the power of His Resurrection, into the seeds of life and love.

That is our hope!

When God is "everything to everyone" (1 Cor 15:28), when our tasks as men and women are finished and we have gone beyond death, we shall understand what now eludes us. Because only then shall we discover the coherence of love and mercy in our lives.

As St. Paul says, "For now we see in a mirror dimly, but then face to face. Now I know in part; then I shall understand fully, even as I have been fully understood. So faith, hope, love abide, these three; but the greatest of these is love" (1 Cor 13: 12-13).

Truly, love triumphs, because it remains for ever.

That is our hope!

IV

'Your Life Is Hid With Christ in God'

In ascending to the right hand of His Father, Jesus reveals what Christian hope is. As the Apostle Paul explains it to the Colossians: "If then you have been raised with Christ, seek the things that are above where Christ is, seated at the right hand of God. Set your mind on things that are above, not on things that are on earth. For you have died and your life is hid with Christ in God" (3:1-3).

This act of faith establishes our hope and its liberating power. Of course, the desire to be recognized and appreciated in this world dwells, in varying degrees, in all of us. How many people complain of being unfairly judged, underestimated, treated with ingratitude! How many more in our image-conscious society set store by appearances! How many young people are fascinated by and want to emulate the look of "stars"! In a word, whether from a concern for impressing certain people, or for fear of what "people might say," or to save face, we live according to the image of ourselves that we want to give to others.

But Christian hope, disclosed by Christ's Ascension, rids us of this enslaving illusion. The worth of our lives is not determined by what others may think about us, by the diplomas acquired, the honors received, the titles accumulated. Whatever we may be able to discern in our lives today is not their ultimate truth. That is hidden with Christ in God. The depth of our lives can be perceived only from above. We must live, not under men's eyes, but exclusively under the eyes of the heavenly Father, "who sees in secret," as Jesus says in the Sermon on the Mount in regard to prayer, fasting, and almsgiving (Mt 6:1ff).

Christ, seated at the right hand of the Father, is presently out of our sight. He is given to us only as a mystery and in the sacraments of the Church. But he is nevertheless leading us with him and is "hiding" away our lives in the Father's secret seeing.

Thus the true dimension of a life, hidden with Christ, is invisible, and will be revealed only when, like Christ, we give ourselves "with love undying" (Eph 6:24). This is why the angels say to the eleven apostles at the time of Christ's ascension: "Men of Galilee, why do you stand looking into heaven? This Jesus, who was taken up from you into heaven will come in the same way as you saw him go into heaven" (Acts 1:11). His appearance at the end of time will be the beginning of his permanent presence in our lives, but until that time he is hidden in us as we are hidden in him. He gives us the strength to face the end of our earthly existence with a hope which is much greater than the sum of all other hopes. This perspective on our lives, seen from above, far from disengaging us, far from taking away all the attraction of the world's ephemeral beauty, gives us the freedom to live here without possessiveness or nostalgia, in a constant state of thanksgiving.

Only those who know that their hidden existence is beyond this world can welcome its precarious splendor. Only those who believe that love is eternal, because they participate in Christ's resurrection, can detect the fleeting glimmer of the good in history, of the grandeur — vanishing so quickly — of each person and each creature, of the noble gestures of human beings and the poetic words they murmur.

If my life is hidden with Christ in God, I can no longer be avidly desirous of anything at all in this world. I cannot regret my passing days or complain about my failures. Who can assess my life except God who loves and saves me?

In his first letter, St. John helps us to understand this hope based on the secret we share with Christ, who has entered into his Father's glory and to whom we presently bear witness:

"See what love the Father has given us, that we should be called children of God; and so we are. The reason why the world does not know us is that it did not know him. Beloved, we are God's children now; it does not yet appear what we shall be, but we know that when he appears we shall be like him, for we shall see him as he is. And every one who thus hopes in him purifies himself as he is pure" (1 Jn 3:1-3).

Truly, the only hope that is worthwhile is to be made holy by our

Lord and Savior, Jesus Christ, the Holy One of God.

"His Ascension is already our victory" as the orison for the Feast of the Ascension says. "We are members of his body, he preceded us in glory next to God, and it is there that we live in hope."

V

The Holy Spirit Gives Us the Strength to Hope

St. Paul [in the French New Testament] speaks of the "deposit" of the Spirit (2 Cor 1:22 and 5:5). The word should not be taken in its current meaning of a "down payment" which can be lost in case a buyer changes his mind. Its meaning is closer to "beginnings." It means that the part given is a "guarantee": whoever possesses the deposit has already, through anticipation, received something of the promised good and is "guaranteed" that he will eventually receive it in its totality.

Again the Apostle Paul writes that we have been "sealed with the promised Holy Spirit, which is the guarantee of our inheritance until we acquire possession of it" (Eph 1:13). Thanks to the Spirit which is given to us, we already possess *in hope* what we shall receive fully at the end of time.

To understand the reality of this hope, take the example of a solitary hiker setting off aimlessly and without a map for a walk through a forest. After a time, the path begins to seem long, and the hope of finding a landmark or a way out becomes more and more fragile. It is a tenuous projection into an uncertain future. But if the hiker meets up with someone who can direct him to the path leading out of the forest, then hope becomes a certitude and drives away fear.

This is the way it is with the Holy Spirit, on whom our hope is based. If, while we are still en route in life's unpredictable journey, we are given by God's grace the deposit of what is going to be granted to us fully in the future, if we receive the strength which allows us to endure, our hope becomes the certainty that we shall eventually receive the remainder of the gift.

By His Spirit, God guides and supports us and makes it possible for us to continue our journey even though the obstacles are numerous, the undergrowth dense, the horizon blocked from view — and our strength diminished.

The very opposite of a pipe dream, Christian hope is a solid reality. It is rooted and sustained in the constant assurance given by the Spirit-Paraclete at work in the present.

Going well beyond a psychological underpinning or the energizing resources of an "optimistic outlook on life," the "virtue" of hope — which is fundamentally the experience of faith — gives the believer the capability of acting immediately, in every situation; and its power is beyond anything we can imagine. It is significant that "Spirit" and "power" are continually associated in Scripture, notably in the Acts of the Apostles. It is in this way that Jesus' promise to his own is accomplished: "But you shall receive power when the Holy Spirit has come upon you" (Acts 1:8).

Here are two examples:

1. In his Gospel, as in his first letter, St. John repeats to us: "God is Love and he wants to abide in us, and we must abide in his love by obeying his commandments." But because of our inability to love, his admonition seems to be out of our reach.

However, the hope of acquiring the virtue of charity does not rest on our present capacity to love. Neither is it a dream of an unblemished generosity in the future. No, our capacity to love — here and now — is a gift of the Holy Spirit, a free gift from God which allows us to overcome our limitations. Jesus' commandment, "Love your enemies", expresses its paradox.

In fact, once the work of Redemption has been completed in our full communion with God, there will be no more enemies, since divine mercy will have reconciled everyone. Jesus' commandment has us experience simultaneously both enmity, with the wounds that it produces, and love, with the forgiveness that causes it to be born. Loving one's enemies (which seems to be contradictory) implies a realistic hope, because only the gift of the Spirit permits us to live this contradiction in its two phases: today, forgiveness at the foot of the Cross; at the end of time, total reconciliation in the glory of the Resurrection.

2. "Pray without ceasing," Jesus exhorts us. But we may as well face it, prayer is often extremely taxing. We have to struggle against

our weaknesses, our refusals, our "little faith." The uninterrupted prayer of the Church, seen at the end of history, is described to us by the visionary of Patmos: "After this I looked, and behold, a great multitude which no man could number, from every nation, from all tribes and peoples and tongues, standing before the throne and before the Lamb, clothed in white robes, with palm branches in their hands, and crying out with a loud voice, 'Salvation belongs to God who sits upon the throne, and to the Lamb!' " (Rev 7:9ff). Nevertheless, Jesus presents prayer to his disciples as a mission and a constant combat.

However, the hope of unceasing prayer rests on the Spirit's strength, not on our own: "Likewise the Spirit helps us in our weakness; for we do not know how to pray as we ought" (Rom 8:26).

Truly, hope never disappoints us, because it is based on the reality of the Spirit's life in our hearts. The Spirit works from within, abides in our prayer and makes our efforts fruitful.

VI

The Secret of Hoping: We Are
United with Christ Redeemer

There are so many dead-end situations in life! How can we offer Christian hope as well as live with it?

Two examples:

A friend of mine has lost his job just one year before his legal retirement age. He wants to fight back, and is looking for work even though his chances of succeeding are slim, if not nil. Why does he do it?

As a Christian, he considers it an act of faith. It is a way of responding to his vocation, of accomplishing his mission by counting on God, not on himself. It is a way of bearing witness to the fact that man cannot be reduced to his calling card or the circumstances which have shaped his social situation. An older person who loses his job is sometimes seriously deprived of material resources, and even more regrettably, he often bears the additional pain of seeing himself discredited by his family and social circle.

Human experience, however, does not end in the world below. The Christian knows that the Holy Spirit dwells within him, and is gradually conforming him to the only Son, dead for our sins and resurrected for our lives. He knows and he asserts that his human dignity does not dry up with the functions that he filled, or with his mortal existence.

His mission as a disciple of Christ cannot be stopped by the tribulations and the ups and downs of life as the Apostle Paul pointed out to the Christians at Corinth: "We are afflicted in every way, but not crushed; perplexed, but not driven to despair; persecuted, but not foresaken; struck down, but not destroyed; always carrying in the body the death of Jesus . . . so that the life of Jesus may be manifested in our mortal flesh" (2 Cor 4:8-10).

The horizon of a person's life does not end with retirement or the grave. It extends to the culmination of human history and the glorious coming of the Son of God. "For he will render to every man according to his works," (Rom 2:6; Ps 62:12), revealing what was hidden in the darkness of time.

Christian hope faces up to the causes of despair, not by suppressing, but by overcoming them. When through faith we bear our suffering as a part of Christ's cross, we then triumph in God's secret.

There is another situation where human hope fails: it is not hard to imagine the distress of someone who, already having experienced the deterioration of his body, finds himself being deprived of his mental faculties. What then is the strength of Christian hope?

The true beauty of life, its meaning, is a secret of which the Christian has received only the deposit through Jesus Christ. And yet what ordeals we have to endure! Sometimes they lead to total despair. What is there to say to someone who is so depressed that the desire to destroy himself completely crushes his will to live?

The person who consents not to turn away from the hope that God gives — the glorious coming of Christ whose "deposit" we have already received by the presence of the Spirit — knows that the suffering of his body or the infirmity of his mind, even if not suppressed, can be transformed.

How?

The Christian can be united with Christ in the worst of trials to which he is subjected, because Christ wishes to bear the sorrows of each of us. It can become a journey of faith, the Way of the Cross.

Remember one of the young martyrs of Lyon who, about to give birth, screams with pain. Her guards ridicule her: "What will you do when you are thrown to the beasts in the arena?" And she replies: "I cry out now because it is I who suffer. But in a little while, Another will be suffering for me."

We, too, can say to our compassionate Lord, "Come bear my burdens, and I will bear Yours. Come take me by the hand. Let me hold Your hand so that Yours will be holding mine."

This then is the secret of Christian hope: whoever participates today in the suffering of the Lord Jesus is united in a hidden way with Christ Redeemer.

He knows that the humiliation of his corporal existence will be "raised" ("resurrected") with the appearance of the Son of Man who has already made us children of God and temples of the Holy Spirit.

You who are presently suffering the humiliation of body, heart and mind, take comfort in the Magnificat of the Virgin Mary: "He has regarded the low estate of his handmaiden . . . and exalted those of low degree."

May the Father of our Lord Jesus Christ bless you richly, you who thirst with the desire of seeing Him and whom He has made to be "born anew to a living hope through the resurrection of Jesus Christ from the dead, and to an inheritance which is imperishable, undefiled and unfading. . ." (1 Pt 1:3-4).

VII

Baptism

It is the sacraments which implant and sustain our hope in Christian truth. First of all, there is baptism.

When parents present their infants for baptism they are dreaming of their future, and are being swept along by a great wave of hope: "Everything is possible." Nevertheless, sooner or later, harsh reality gets the upper hand: failures, difficulties, and disappointments of all sorts occur and the dream begins to fray.

This is bound to happen to a certain extent because a child is *himself*, and not some ideal his parents have envisaged. But there are also other reasons: adversity can strike, bringing physical or mental suffering for the child. His character may be weak. He may even revolt against his parents and his upbringing and eventually reject them. . . . So many parents have confided their sorrows to me, sorrows which are inconsolable: a son who wished to dedicate his life to God is struck down in the flower of his youth; another, past thirty, lets go of everything, as though he has completely lost his bearings.

How is it possible, when parents are disappointed by reality, to go on living with the hope they had when their children were baptized?

Was their hope only an illusion growing out of the naiveté of their youth? A futile pipe dream? No, because Christian hope goes much further. In bringing a child into the world, parents transmit life according to the flesh. But by the Sacrament of Baptism, they transmit the life of God.

In the act of baptism, the broad outlines of an infant's future are already astonishingly visible: he has become a child of God, he shares the dignity of Christ — priest, prophet, and king — and he is a Temple of the Holy Spirit. Although the details of his future are unknown, his vocation is not. What lies ahead of him downstream cannot be predicted; but upstream, he has received the call that faith knows with certitude: the call to his vocation.

No matter what happens later, he has been called to be Christ's brother in this world; henceforth, he is to witness to the love and mercy of God, he is to be a messenger of the Good News.

Like Mary at the Annunciation, we ask, "How shall this be?" The answer, even for the saints, escapes us. We cannot relate the complete truth of their lives as God alone sees them! Who can know the greatness of a hidden love, measure the value of dry tears, perceive the solidity and secret beauty of any human being's existence? No one, except God.

Parents who have asked for their child's baptism receive the certitude of his or her Christian vocation, and they can carry within themselves an indestructible hope, because they can and must call on God, who irrevocably keeps His word. Whatever the situation of your child, whatever his erring ways, since by the pure grace of God he has been baptized in the death and Resurrection of Christ and made similar to the Son, God will give him the staying power to fulfill his vocation and to make his life serve for the world's salvation. Invisibly, but definitely — even if this accomplishment remains incomprehensible to you who possibly will never live to witness it.

Remember what the Apostle Peter writes to the first Christians: "You have been born anew, not of perishable seed but of imperishable, through the living and abiding word of God; for 'All flesh is like grass and all its glory like the flower of grass. The grass withers, and the flower falls, but the word of the Lord abides for ever.' That word is the good news which was preached to you. . . . Therefore gird up your minds, be sober, set your hope fully upon the grace that is coming to you at the revelation of Jesus Christ" (1 Pt 1:23-25, 13).

These words, then, are the foundation of parents' hope when they present their child for baptism. From that moment, they know the essential secret of a life whose intricate pattern will escape them in this world. Only in the heavenly kingdom will they, along with everyone else, discover "the mystery of his will, according to his purpose which he set forth in Christ as a plan for the fulness of time, to unite all things in him, things in heaven and things on earth'' (Eph 1:9-10).

You who have been baptized, who are distressed and discouraged when you measure the abyss between the ambitious plans of your youth and your desperate failures, you must look back on the grace of your baptism. What parents have to repeat to themselves in faith and hope about their children, you — adults confirmed in the Holy Spirit — must all the more so repeat to yourselves.

Your baptism in Christ is the source of the hope you can have for yourself, and it is God's hope for you. Whatever may have happened in your life, the essential — your baptismal vocation — remains. That is a hope that no one can take away from you, because ''God is faithful, by whom you were called into the fellowship of his Son, Jesus Christ our Lord'' (1 Cor 1:9).

VIII

The Eucharist

Every Christian knows from experience: the Eucharist is the vital nourishment for children of God.

The hope that the Eucharist brings us cannot be reduced to a little extra strength to help us continue on our way — like the cake that the angel placed beside an exhausted and discouraged Elijah on the road to Mount Horeb: "Arise and eat, else the journey will be too great for you" (1 Kings 19:6-7), or like the manna sent to the Hebrews in the desert (Exodus 16:4ff). At the synagogue in Capernaum Jesus underlines the difference between the two types of nourishment: "Your fathers ate the manna in the wilderness and they died. This is the bread which came down from heaven . . . if any one eats of this bread, he will live for ever; and the bread which I shall give for the life of the world is my flesh" (Jn 6:31ff).

To discover how the Eucharist nourishes our hope, we have only to listen to St. Paul. After having recalled its institution by the Lord Jesus, he declares: "For as often as you eat this bread and drink this cup, you proclaim the Lord's death until he comes" (1 Cor 11:23).

The Eucharist orients us toward the glorious coming of our Lord. At the same time, it is the presence in our lives, day after day, of what Christ accomplished two thousand years ago in Jerusalem — at the Last Supper, on the Cross and at his Resurrection — for our redemption. And it gives us a foretaste of what will come to pass at the end of time, as if we were living the present moment with both arms outstretched, touching the two extremities of the world's history. Whence comes that haste, that impatience that the Christian sometimes feels: "Come, Lord Jesus!" writes the prophet of Patmos in concluding the book of Revelation (22:20). Like the runner in the stadium, the apostle is "straining forward to what lies ahead," according to Paul's description (cf. Phil 3:13). This interior tension between the two poles, joyfully derived from the Eucharist, sustains our Christian hope.

In partaking of the Eucharist we are able to possess in part what we are hoping to receive eventually in plenitude — because in communing with the Body of the resurrected Christ, we are already sharing in the Resurrection. The bread and wine changed into the Body and Blood of Christ (transubstantiation) attest that already God is seizing — from the interior — the corporal, historical existence of creation to make of it the sacrament of life transfigured by the power of the Holy Spirit. Already, our pathetic bodies, which will nevertheless know the corruption of death, are inhabited by the imperishable seed of eternity and resurrection (cf. 1 Pt 1:23).

At present, the eucharistic mystery is at the center of the universe's transfiguration, a transfiguration given by grace, as if the beauty of the world is being pierced from the interior by God's regard. Yes, even our broken and ailing bodies, our shattered and sinful existences are transfigured by the Eucharist. It gives us the strength to hope for the definitive fulfillment of what is already being given to us in the relativity of our corporal condition. This hope belongs not to the realm of imagination, but to the realm of belief. How could we believe in the future resurrection if we had not already experienced it in the Eucharist? Our hope and our faith in the reestablishment — in Christ — of all humanity and the entire universe (cf. Acts 3:21) is based on a reality of the here and now: the real Presence of the resurrected Christ in the sacred species of bread and wine.

In the Eucharist, we experience the conclusion of the journey while we are still on the road. How powerful our hope is!

The Eucharist is a communion of charity. How beautiful our hope is!

The Eucharist transforms Christians — "Become what you receive" — and providing that they recognize Christ as the source of their unity and the Church as his unique body, it unites in the Body of Christ men and women whom everything else can separate. The Eucharist heals divisions since it reconciles sinners with God and their brothers by giving them the grace to be gathered into the unique body of Christ.

Not only does the Eucharist give us the strength to love, it also allows us to anticipate the time when "God may be everything to everyone" (1 Cor 15:28). The history of the human species will not end with its disappearance from the earth's surface. It will terminate only when in the fullness of time a multitude of brothers and sisters are united in a communion of love under a single Head, Christ.

In every celebration of the Eucharist, our communion is already giving birth to this body, and this body is giving birth to us. How marvelous our hope is!

IX

Matrimony

What is hope for those who ask for and receive the sacrament of matrimony?

According to statistics, one-third of all marriages in France (one-half for the Paris area) risk terminating in divorce within the first three years. Young people who approach matrimony have to say to themselves: "There is one chance in three that our marriage will fail!" Faced with such a prospect, Christian hope for marital success appears very tenuous indeed.

Moreover, among those who attempt the "adventure," many are dreaming of a mutual understanding, a complete openess — in a word, of a passionate love that time can never destroy. The relationship of a man and a woman idealized to such a point becomes a chimera, a utopia. However well matched two people may be, they will eventually wound each other. It is normal — inevitable — that conjugal love is just as difficult to live as charity, because it is, after all, a form of it. And charity is always crucifying.

Are these considerations pessimistic? No, simply realistic, in order to specify the conditions in which a marital union can be envisaged with hope. Besides, there would be a great deal to say about the often distressing experience of couples who refuse the institution of marriage. Our epoch has destabilized relations between men and women. The sufferings born from an unmarried lifestyle are often greater than those caused by the constraints which formerly anchored married couples in a greater constancy.

What hope then can a bride and groom bring to the sacrament of matrimony? Many couples have the vague feeling that the sacrament will give them a supplementary chance for success. The benediction of God, they reason, will bestow a sacred character to their union,

41

and hence, *guarantee* their desire for fidelity and happiness. They realize that they are vulnerable; they know their limitations; and they have witnessed so many failures all around them. So they look to God to give them the assurance that human strength is incapable of giving.

This, however, is not the function of the Sacrament of Matrimony. The function of this rite is to transfigure the union of a man and a woman at the same time that it makes precise demands: the union is to be unique, indissoluble, open to fertility. The couple must be ready not only to help each other in the ordinary conditions of existence, but also, and especially, to work for each other, through each other, in the accomplishment of their divine vocations. In brief, the Sacrament of Matrimony establishes a couple's call to sainthood. *That* is to be their vocation.

Like all sacraments, it is the spiritual symbol of a divine reality given to mankind. In the circumstances, conjugal love becomes not only the symbol, but the sacrament of God's union with His people, and of Christ's union with His Church. In the Book of Revelation, St. John shows us how in the Church "the marriage of the Lamb has come and his Bride has made herself ready" (Rev 19:7). And St. Paul says of the marital union: "This is a great mystery, and I mean in reference to Christ and his church" (Eph 5:32).

Through the sacrament of matrimony, a man and a woman are given the possibility of living their lives together with the strength of Christ-Redeemer, who loves his Church and abides in their union. But even so, they receive no guarantees that difficulties can be avoided. What they do receive is the firm hope of being able to cope with them through recourse to the grace of Christ, each day of their lives. Christ, who "loved the Church and gave himself up for her, that he might sanctify her, having cleansed her by the washing of water with the word, that he might present the church to himself in splendor, without spot or wrinkle or any such thing, that she might be holy and without blemish" (Eph 5:25-27), makes it possible for two people, delivered from their sins, to forgive each other, to endure life's more or less cruel trials, and also to know the joy and holiness of the gift of oneself and shared love.

You who are living in the conjugal state, sometimes in sorrow and darkness, are able to give these words all their resonance!

Those who live with this sacramental grace also receive the hope that at the end of their lives, brought together with everyone in communion with God, they will taste the happiness of the Bridegroom, Christ, and of His Bride, the Church.

The Christian hope which is linked with the Sacrament of Matrimony gives the couple a superhuman strength for their daily life, and allows them to go forward with a perspective which surpasses our earthly horizon.

The union of a man and woman cannot be reduced to the limited goal of a "happiness" which each partner is free to explore and then abandon when he grows weary of it. It is inscribed in the divine vocation of every person who enters it that "the Spirit and the Bride say" to the Bridegroom, "Come" (Rev 22:17).

X

Ordination

By the Sacrament of Holy Orders, we discover the nature of the hope we have in the Church.

Superficially, the bishops, priests and deacons who have been ordained might be likened to the hierarchical system that exists in any company or institution. But there is a radical difference: they have been "constituted" by the mission that Jesus first entrusted to the apostles; they act "in the name of Jesus" throughout the course of history.

After the confession of Simon, son of John, at Caesarea Philippi, the Lord said to him: "You are Peter, and on this rock I will build my church" (Mt 16:18-19). Thus Christ founded His Church on Peter (and his successors, the Popes) and on the college of apostles (and their successors, the bishops). They are "pillars" of the Church (Gal 2:9), that "spiritual temple" made up of "living stones" (1 Pt 2:4).

The apostles, including Peter as their head, will be tempted by power, just as all hierarchies are, whether military, civil or administrative. . . . To warn the twelve about this temptation, to make them understand the nature of their apostolic mission, Christ compares it to a slave's service. During the Last Supper, He washes their feet (cf. Jn 13:4-16), and He says to them expressly: "You know that the rulers of the Gentiles lord it over them, and their great men exercise authority over them. It shall not be so among you; but whoever would be great among you must be your servant, and whoever would be first among you must be your slave; even as the Son of man came not to be served but to serve, and to give his life as a ransom for many" (Mt 20: 25-28).

To Peter, whom he has just instituted head of His Church, Christ promises that "the powers of death shall not prevail against it." He is not predicting that the Church will be sheltered from great trials — that would be contrary to historical evidence. In fact, He warns His apostles: " 'A servant is not greater than his master.' If they persecuted me, they will persecute you" (Jn 15:20; cf. Mt 10:32). And again, He quotes from the prophet Zechariah: "I will strike the shepherd, and the sheep will be scattered" (Mk 14:27).

The Lord does not envisage the Church's future as a human triumph: "I have said this to you, that in me you may have peace. In the world you have tribulation; but be of good cheer, I have overcome the world" (Jn 16:33). Jesus is announcing that His Church will share in his victory over death, in His Resurrection.

The sacrament of Holy Orders, an effective sign of apostolic continuity in the Church throughout history, gives the Church the sacramental assurance which constitutes her. Therefore, she is never enclosed in her own realization at any specific epoch or place. Although she is a part of history, she crosses and transcends it. In a changing world, she expresses God's fidelity to His plan for universal salvation. That is why the Church can already dispense the goods of the future.

Through the sacrament of ordination, the Pope, bishops, priests and deacons are given by God to the Church, to men and women whom God has called for the visible constitution of the body of Christ. Their ordination is a reminder to the faithful that what they are experiencing, what brings them together and makes their unity, surpasses the present moment and their power. The beauty of the Church is that she is completely braced for that future time when she will receive in full the goods whose guarantee she holds already.

Hence, ordained ministers are the witnesses to the kingdom to come. They act as guarantors for the truth that holiness is not exhausted by what men experience, that the tears of the poor, the suffering of the just, the prayer of the chosen associated with the Redeemer, save the world and bring about the conversion of hearts.

The sacrament of ordination is the Church's guarantee that the Word announced today is the eternal Word of God; that the Charity consisting of forgiveness and compassion is much greater than all the divisions among Christians; that the love that dwells in the Church "never ends" (1 Cor 13:8); that it is not our solidarity alone which forms the body of Christ: it is also formed by the communion that God creates among all men, through Christ, with Christ, in Christ.

Loving the Church and preserving her unity is the role of her shepherds, servants of the unique Shepherd, Christ, who "lays down his life for the sheep" and comes 'to gather into one the children of God who are scattered abroad" (Jn 10:11, 11:52). That is why Jesus warns the apostles against the "false prophets, who come to you in sheep's clothing, but inwardly are ravenous wolves" (Mt 7:15).

At this very moment, the Church is bearing witness to the resurrection of the dead and the victory of love over death and sin. The sacraments we receive are the evidence of this. And we have the sacraments thanks to the ministry of the priests who are in communion with the apostolic college — from age to age.

The Church is a *living* hope!

XI

Mercy

The sacrament of mercy [penance or reconciliation] was instituted by Christ as His first gift to His Church. The Church is its servant, the priest its minister. Through the confession of our sins we are repeatedly delivered from our weaknesses and secret wretchedness. We are able to rediscover the plenitude of life from God received at baptism. But this spiritual experience, so characteristic of Catholicism, does not express all the magnanimity of this sacrament or all the hope of which it is the guarantee.

When we confess our sins, God gives us the grace — stunning! — to perceive what sin, *our* sin, is: a negation, a refusal of God. Whoever receives such an enlightenment acknowledges with terror that God is ''justified in thy sentence and blameless in thy judgment'' (Ps 51:4). The sinner knows that according to God's truth, he does not deserve to be forgiven.

But when we take the step of returning our hearts to God, He also gives us the grace — overflowing with hope! — to realize that His forgiveness is never merited. It is a true miracle, a sign of infinite love of which we shall always remain unworthy. Through the sacrament of mercy, we become aware once more of just how little and how poorly we love, and of how undeserved and immeasurable is the love that God brings to us in His Son, Jesus.

No one, except Christ (cf. 2 Cor 5:21), can say that he is without sin: ''If we say we have no sin, we deceive ourselves, and the truth is not in us'' (cf. 1 Jn 1:8). But in Christ, who was ''made to be sin,'' all men are called to recognize that they are sinners who are loved and forgiven.

What magnanimity and hope there is in the sacrament of mercy!

It goes even deeper, however. The sacrament in which we confess our sins is much more than a mere succor to pick us up when

47

we have stumbled, to set us back on the road when we have come to a halt or to open us up to God's light when our obstinacy has walled us into darkness. It gives us something much more conclusive: God willing — and God is willing! — it gives us the hope of our eternal salvation. Regardless of how numerous and serious they are, all the things that make us feel guilty cannot prevent God from wanting to save us until the very end of our lives. The sacrament of mercy gives us the hope that we shall not be ultimately lost, "damned."

In contemporary society, most people hesitate to use the word "damnation." But why should they, after all, since we are constantly encountering temporal illustrations of eternal damnation? I am thinking of all those people who, secretly despairing both in themselves *and* in God, commit suicide not only by attacking their physical lives, but by annihilating themselves spiritually — with drugs, alcohol, perverted passions, etc. . . .

In a sense, whoever lives in our world without any hope of salvation or is even content to say "What's the point?" — whoever simply throws up his hands — has already condemned himself. To be damned is to damn oneself. God never condemns us (cf. Jn 3: 17 and 1 Jn 3:20) as long as we continue to ask for and accept His forgiveness which saves and heals us.

The sacrament of mercy is humiliating only to the person who does not accept being freely loved by God. It is the sacrament of an indestructible hope based on the disinterested love that God has for each of us, a love that goes well beyond the limits of our terrestial and visible life.

Just as the future of the newly baptized is uncertain — while his vocation is not — our chaotic lives conceal from our eyes their coherent courses and their beauty. The sacrament of mercy adds Christian hope to them: every person's existence culminates in God's love and forgiveness, which give it its consistency and splendor.

No life is ever lost or ruined. Never. You may feel that you have failed in your marriage, your job as a parent, your professional life, etc. But *you* are much more than those successive missions which were entrusted to you. The secret beauty of your life escapes you.

You cannot judge it. It is the love that God has for you. Yes, for you —just as you are. By the sacrament of mercy, this love is progressively revealed to us throughout our lives.

Far from being the perpetual and exhausting "patching up" of a failed life which one attempts to "salvage" the way one "salvages" a handmade mayonnaise, the grace of this sacrament works from deep within to "finish" us so that we bear a likeness to God, our Creator. Each time that we receive forgiveness, we are touched by the chisel with which, little by little, God cleanses us, and like the vessel of clay that was spoiled in the potter's hand, we are reworked by God's hands to reflect His image (Jer 18:6). God, our Father, gives his beauty to our souls, he shapes the faces of his children. We become ourselves because God loves us and wants us to love Him.

"Beloved, we are God's children now; it does not yet appear what we shall be, but we know that when he appears we shall be like him, for we shall see him as he is. And every one who thus hopes in him purifies himself as he is pure" (1 Jn 3:2-3).

'You Shall Love
The Lord Your God'*

This series of seven sermons echoes Thomas à Kempis in the Imitation of Christ. *It turns the believer in the only possible direction — toward the Lord God. As the fifteenth-century guide announces with the directness that characterizes Cardinal Lustiger: "God alone, who is eternal and incomprehensible, is the whole solace and comfort of the soul."*

There is no talk here of an easy, soothing road to the Lord, no evasive discussion that ignores the magnitude of the Lord's call, no facile rhetoric filled with shortcuts. Here it is, Christians, says the Cardinal, here is the word of God — "You shall love the Lord your God."

What that means — believing, answering the call, passing it on to succeeding generations, and, above all, loving and hoping — is captured in preaching that laces its encouraging words with realism. All of this is presented with emphasis on the Lord as the God of life and of living, a source of strength as well as solace.

---

* These sermons, delivered on Radio Notre-Dame between September 4 and October 23, 1985, were translated by John Laughlin, Our Sunday Visitor, Inc., book editor.

I

You Shall Teach
It to Your Children

The commandments of God: God entrusts His life to us and calls us to act like Him, divinely.

"Be imitators of God," writes St. Paul to the Christians of Ephesus (5:1), "as beloved children." Far from being an excessive, arbitrary constraint imposed on humanity, the commandments of God — because they are *of God*, "the Source of life " — give our lives all their fullness and all their beauty as the lives of children of God. In fact, fulfilling the commandments through the gift of the Holy Spirit makes us enter into communion with the Father in His Son.

"Every one, then, who hears these words of mine and does them," Jesus reminds us at the end of the Sermon on the Mount, "will be like a wise man who built his house upon the rock..." (Mt 7:24). To "put into practice" what God wants and to do it with the strength of the Holy Spirit means becoming one with Christ, conqueror of sin and of death.

* * *

The "commandments," gathered in "ten words," are given in two "tablets": the first with regard to God, the second with regard to neighbor. During these sermons, I propose that you meditate on *the commandments with regard to God* (Ex 20:1-6; cf. also Dt 5:6-10).

To begin, the first commandment: "*I am the LORD your God, who brought you out* of the land of Egypt, out of the house of bondage. You shall have no other gods before me. You will not make for yourself a graven image..." (Ex 20:2-4).

51

Deuteronomy (6:1-9) condenses the commandments of the first tablet in a phrase constantly repeated by Israel, by Jesus (Mk 12:30; cf. also Mt. 22-27, Lk 10:27):

"Hear, O Israel: The LORD our God is one LORD; and you shall love the Lord your God with all your heart, and with all your soul, and with all your mind, and with all your might. . . . And these words which I command you . . . you shall teach them diligently to your children, and shall talk of them when you sit in your house, and when you walk by the way, and when you sit down, and when you rise" (Dt 6:4-5, 7).

* * *

What questions does this first commandment pose for us today, in this society marked by unbelief and atheism?

How can we *receive as a commandment of God* to love Him when one cannot be forced to believe in Him?

How can we *transmit* this commandment to succeeding generations when they say they don't believe? That is one of the fundamental questions of our era. How many parents, how many grandparents have felt a pang in their hearts upon hearing these words of the Bible only to declare: "My God, my children, my little ones, what have they become? Why have they lost the Faith? . . ."

What is at stake is considerable: the happiness, the life, much more, the salvation of humanity. It is important not to minimize the fact that it is *a commandment* of God and not to downplay the difficulty of observing it. The commandments toward the neighbor can seem to us easier to put into practice. But in truth, the character, the fine point of Christian conduct of humans toward one another, is oriented, commanded, *established by this relation of each human* and of all humans *with regard to God.*

It all holds together. The drama of the world, the drama of men and women among themselves, is also the drama of humanity, the drama of men facing God. To the question "Which commandment is the first of all?" (Mk 12:28) Jesus replies by refusing to choose "the first," "the principal" commandment. He tells us that they *all* hold together and that *all* are to be realized (Mt 5:17-20). That *all together* they put us into love. And that it is not possible to be truly faithful to the one without being faithful to the other. Is this easy? Is it possible?

It is the whole point of the Gospel. Paradox and hope.

II

A Call to Believe: to Follow Jesus

To understand the first commandment of God, we listen to Jesus in the Gospel of Mark (10:17ff):

To the rich man who asks of Him, "Good teacher, what must I do to inherit eternal life?" He replies, "Why do you call me good? No one is good but God alone," an implicit quotation from Israel's profession of faith (Dt 6:4): "The LORD our God is *one LORD.*" Jesus follows up: "You know the commandments . . ." and there are enumerated the commandments with regard to neighbor: "Teacher, all these I have observed from my youth." Jesus then adds: "You lack one thing," which is meant to say: observing the commandments that concern the love and service of God, the first commandment. "Go, sell what you have, and give to the poor . . . and come, follow me."

Jesus loves this man. Gazing at him, He invites him to let everything go so that his treasure may be God Himself. He calls him to walk in His steps, to do what He does, in brief, *to act as a child of God in following Him, the Son of God.* For only the unique Son perfectly adores, loves, serves the unique Father.

* * *

To follow Christ, to walk behind Him toward His Passion, is also what Jesus teaches in order to observe the first commandment.

This teaching of Jesus seems less surprising to us if we return to the text of Exodus (20:2): "*I am the LORD your God, who brought* you out of the land of Egypt, out of the house of servitude." Before giving these "ten words," God calls Himself by His own unpronounceable name, "the LORD (YWVH) your God." He makes himself ours in the revelation he confides about Himself.

God calls to man so that man can respond to him. His creative

54

word renders man answerable. Not like a tyrant who would demand gratitude for his gifts, but like a Father without whom we would not be, God controls love because, first, He has the initiative of love, love that awakens to existence.

God also presents Himself in the prodigious action that saved his people, oppressed in Egypt and enslaved by sin. The commandment of God begins with a commitment of God with regard to these whom He invites to communicate with His holy will. In a sovereign act of freedom, He brings His people "out of the house of bondage." He gives humanity its freedom, of which the first commandment traces the narrow track: freedom recovered, wrenched away by the power of the love of God from the powers of slavery and death.

* * *

"You shall have no strange gods before me" (Ex 20:3). These other gods do not give out their names themselves. And with cause: they are "nothing," "nothings," the prophets will say. It is man who procures them as gods. Whereas the Lord makes man exist in his own image and makes him free.

People who would accept this commandment are under the gaze of God, "before Him." God, in calling them to this face-to-face encounter, has unveiled something of Himself. And to observe this commandment of God is for man to respond to his vocation.

Two immediate consequences:

To present for baptism a child who is going to be born is to acknowledge the initiative of God, who wants to give to a little human the freedom of a child of God. By what right deprive him or her of that grace of which you parents have been providentially the object?

To reflect on your baptism received when quite young—in freely making an act of faith — is to recognize in your own history a providential call that marks your existence as a human being.

Far from being an anonymous number, interchangeable in a series, and despite the illusion of genetic manipulations, each one is born individual, irreplaceable. Although they may not choose their birth or parents, their language, their country, their era, all humans come into the world providentially in the grand design of God.

A Call to Believe: God Goes Before Us

Can God oblige us to believe in Him? This seems contradictory to us. Nevertheless, isn't this what the first commandment of God asks of us? To think thus is not to understand the why in which God calls us to relations with Him. For then we would be examining ourselves on the existence of God like astrophysicists polling themselves on the existence of a hypothetical star. Thus would it be a discovery of God at the end of man's reasoning.

"Whether God exists or not has no effect on my life," say certain people today, like the ancient fool of the Bible (cf. Ps 14:1, 53:2). "In the pride of his countenance the wicked man does not seek him [God]; all his thoughts are, 'There is no God' " (Ps 10:4). Man, then, takes no interest in anything except himself — "me, me, me" — and the mirror in which he contemplates his image sends him back into total solitude. "If not for me, then, no one loves me. Then what good is living?" he says in his blindness. His life is a night in which he hides from God.

* * *

Well, the first commandment does not ask that man acquire a conviction about God from the first, but that he *accepts being situated facing an initiative of God*. He does not begin either with an order ("You will do this") or with a prohibition ("You will not do that"), but with a revelation: "I am the LORD your God, who brought you out of the land of Egypt, out of the house of bondage" (Dt 5:6). And the act of faith consists in recognizing the One who first reveals Himself to us, delivers us, and gives Himself to us.

Faith in the One who alone is God *is a grace*. That doesn't mean that God one day sends forth an irresistible illumination that reduces faith to an irrational passion. On the contrary, faith is grace because it is gift of enlightenment, of wisdom.

God turns our heart in such a way that we would open our eyes and discover Him. He who was already there without our knowing, who had already stated His name, who had called us beforehand and taken us by the hand.

The intellect needs to assert itself so that this discovery finds all its consistency and its sense. It must clear the road leading toward God, whose call we have heard in a manner more or less implicit. The grace of faith precedes the call of God, which at the same time gives our reason the ability to understand the words of wisdom through which God reveals Himself. It gives our freedom the strength to be disengaged from its sin and to cling to the love of God in adoration and the action of grace. God is at the edge — because He is at the origin — and our spirit stretches toward Him.

* * *

Discovery of the opening act of God in my regard, the adherence of faith, *common to adulthood*, is at the same time the discovery that I play the part of those whom he has called and assembled. To ask for baptism is to take part in the initiative of God's love for all mankind.

Not to baptize an infant for fear of attacking his freedom is to *resist the freedom of God*. In giving that child to you, baptized parents, God wishes to give him the freedom of the children of God and to open a way of life for him. Far from constraining the freedom of mankind, God frees it, awakens it and draws it from the shadows where it slumbers in order to take it, through baptism, to the day of the Sun of God, in Jesus Christ, the "day" that will "dawn upon us from on high" (Lk 1:78).

The first commandment addressed to man is the converse of the initiative of God. Just as God says His Name to His people and delivers them, so each is invited to reply to him by an act of faith, to place his heart naked before Him, to offer his liberty of love, his soul to adore the sole and unique Lord.

IV

A Call to Love: 'You Look For Me'

To observe the first commandment of God is to respond to God not only through faith but also through love. If it is not possible for you to believe serenely in God, courage brothers and sisters, don't give up searching or loving. "Seeking the LORD while he may be found" (Is 55:6). In fact, the Lord has said, "When you seek me with all your heart, I will be found by you" (Jer 29:13-14). His love is kind (cf. 1 Jn 4:19). But it is exacting. More than the apostles are able to conceive. Peter is shocked that the Messiah has to suffer and die. Jesus reproves him: "*Your thoughts are not those of God but those of men*" (Mk: 8:27ff).

To believe God, to love God, is to enter into the thought and plan of God. That obliges us to follow Jesus, the well-beloved Son of the Father. He enters without reserve into the designs of God, wresting us from the mortal solitude of sin.

To believe God, to love God, is to come forward on one's own to recognize the One through whom we exist. Faith and charity are *the response in the heart of man to the creative and saving love of God*. See why it is vital to observe this first commandment. To escape from it is to die. To reconcile your thoughts to the thoughts of God, with Christ, thanks to the Holy Spirit, is to live.

* * *

It is necessary to love God; for love. In our time, in our civilization, often love is devaluated. It is reduced to sexuality, deprived of all spiritual significance. It is reduced to emotional experience, intense, precarious, fragile, never assured of enduring. And yet it is a unique reality of love that appertains to human dignity. Faced with the decay of *amorous expectation* — note I say expectation, not experience — man may then believe in true love, the only remedy: to discover that love comes from God; better, that "God is love" (1 Jn 4:8).

For man, created in the image of God and called to communion with God, love is bearer of the divine. Knowing that God loves him, he will know what it means to love: to love God, to love his brothers and sisters. To discover the beauty of a conjugal and familial love rooted in the fidelity of God. To understand the splendor of chastity for the Kingdom, sign of love without measure given through Christ.

* * *

What does it mean to love God, whom I do not see, do not touch, do not hear — God who is imperceptible and transcendent? And how do I know if I love God?

To this call, most often disconcerting, to love God, however, it is necessary to *answer yes.* Like Jeremiah: "You have seized me, LORD; you have been the mightiest"; like Hosea, Amos and the other prophets. Like Peter, of whom the Risen Jesus asks, after three exceptional years of living together in enthusiasm and in tears: "Do you love me more than these?" Like Paul, brought by the One whom he has persecuted to a state of power: "I live by faith in the Son of God, who loved me and gave himself for me" (Gal 2:20).

Like the innumerable saints who have spoken so eloquently of their love for God. Thus spoke Sister Thérèse Couderc, founder of the Notre Dame congregation of the Cenacle. Totally dedicated to the love of God, she confided at her death (whose centennial we are celebrating): "What does it matter if my naked and lacerated feet should fill my wooden shoes with blood, I would gladly start out again on my way; *so happy have I been to find God.*"

Yes, it is a human experience of the love of God, tangible among the prophets, the apostles, the saints. But what about us?

V

A Call to Love: 'And You Shall Know Me'

Can one truly love God as a bridegroom loves his bride, a child his father? *Yes and no.* For our poor love — fleeting, vulnerable, unstable — is only an obscure reflection, a hazy image of the love that is God. The love of God in the purest truth moves all human existence and ushers it into the fullness of communion with the God who is love. No more the unceasing threat to man's encounter with his Creator and Redeemer.

It is not starting with us but with God that we will truly know how to love. God alone teaches us to love, in loving us "even to the end" in His Son. While human love seems to help in understanding the love of God, the believer discovers in *the grace of God's love* the source and the absolute foundation of human love.

This first commandment to love God above all things, to love him as he loves us, is a *flash of light* that illumines, comforts the precariousness, the deficiencies, the infidelity of our love. At the same time, it opens up the unsuspected horizon of God's love endlessly offered, of tenderness lavished without measure.

* * *

It is the same experience of the people of Israel, described so vigorously by the prophet Hosea. The love of God for His people is compared to the love *of a husband for his wife*. That unfaithful wife sells her beauty, which comes to her nevertheless from God's love (cf. Hos 2:4ff). Love so great and so powerful that God will restore to the disfigured wife her original beauty and fidelity.

It is also compared to the love *of a father for his child*. The child escapes from the one who gives him life, guards him in life: "When Israel was a child I loved him, and out of Egypt I called my son. . . . They kept sacrificing to the Baals. . . . Yet it was I who taught Ephraim to walk. They did not know that I healed them. I led them

60

with the bonds of love, and I became for them as one who eases the yoke on their jaws" (Hos 11:1-4).

* * *

Thus, this first commandment with regard to God reveals to man that he does not love, does not know, cannot love God, who does not cease loving. Is it to imprison him in his denial? To reproach him for his lack of love? To crush him with nostalgia for an ideal impossible to attain. No. God takes man out of the egotism in which he chokes, from his spiritual "autism," this drama of sinning man, made for love, remaining a prisoner of his "heart of stone" (Ez 11:19).

"You shall love the LORD your God, who brought you out of the land of Egypt": this commandment of God allows man to discover God's love, which makes him *be born* to the life of a child of God, in the unique and well-loved Son (cf. Jn 1:12). Did not Jesus say, "Unless you turn and become like little children . . . (Mt 18:3)?

The love of God expresses itself at the highest point in the gift of His Son: "God so loved the world that he gave his only Son, that whoever believes in him should not perish but have eternal life" (Jn 3:16). And the Apostle Paul explains to the Christians of Rome: "One will hardly die for a righteous man — though perhaps for a good man one will dare even to die. But God shows his love for us in that while we were yet sinners Christ died for us" (Rom 5:7-8).

Man, through love, can sacrifice himself even to self-destruction, at least from a human viewpoint. God Himself cannot but live and give life. In His love, the gift of His Son even to death on the cross is not the destruction of the Son but *His glorification and the birth of all the children* redeemed by the blood of the crucified and risen Messiah.

* * *

God teaches us that love is superabundant fertility and absolute fidelity: "I will betroth you to me for ever; I will betroth you to me in justice and righteousness, in steadfast love and in mercy. I will betroth you to me in faithfulness, and you shall know the LORD" (Hos 2:19-20).

VI

A Call to Hope: 'Against All Hope'

To live the first commandment with regard to God is to believe in Him, to love Him. But it is also *to hope* in Him. To many, this seems even *more difficult*, more challenging. We are considered optimists or pessimists — at the same time a reproach and a compliment—according to the viewpoint we bring to the events of life or of the world. As if we were not capable of accepting reality in its often cruel diversity.

Does the hope that God gives us and asks of us consist of being assured that such-and-such a matter is going to turn out well because we have done all that we could and trusted in the Providence of God? Indeed, "your heavenly Father knows that you need..." (Mt 6:32). And every event can become "providential," a source of love.

But hope does not consist in imagining that God is going to give us this or that, to satisfy our desires, as perhaps a spoiled child. That would confuse hope with the ephemeral satisfaction of covetousness, albeit to remedy a difficulty. Even if you get what you desire, life will remain uncertain. Then it would be necessary to endure new disappointments. That is not hoping in God. In running after your desires, your life is in the process of *withering*, like a dead leaf, like a faded flower. Whereas *the measure of your life* is *God Himself*.

In situations hopeless to human eyes (accidents, irreversible illness, death, separation, etc.), to encourage hope is not to speak fine words. Neither is it to deny an ordeal and its unavoidable character, nor to deny fear. It is to have *a hope stronger* than despair, hope that allows us not to suppress it but to endure it, thanks to *faith in the love that God brings us.*

* * *

To hope in God is not a matter of temperament, enterprising and never depressive. Certain people carry within themselves a sadness without remedy, living with a wounded psyche. Will they be less near to God and will they prove less hopeful than those who enjoy an unalterable optimism? God cannot make an obligation of what does not depend on us: our temperament or the circumstances in which we find ourselves.

To hope in God is to let our life expand, to take the measure of a life that relies uniquely upon God, all Love and the Source of Life. It is not a matter of hoping for this or that, but of recognizing that God is the Lord who has wrested us from bondage. From that time, each day, our life acquires an unprecedented, irreplaceable splendor that appears as such even to eyes brimming with tears.

Without ever being a compensation—since humiliating injustice, derided love do not bear easy compensation — this hope does not deceive. It enables man to face the cruelest of tests.

Like the Apostle Paul, who dared to write to the Christians of Corinth, ''We are afflicted in every way, but not crushed; perplexed, but not driven to despair; persecuted, but not forsaken; struck down, but not destroyed; always carrying in the body the death of Jesus, so that the life of Jesus may be manifested in our mortal flesh'' (2 Cor 4:8-10).

Christ tells us the value of hope, He who knows the burdens of evil and takes it to the point of crying out on the cross, ''My God, my God, *why hast thou forsaken me*?'' (Mt 27:48).

But from this most profound cry of despair (cf. Ps 22:1-2, there bursts the most powerful prayer of hope: ''Father, *into thy hands* I commit my spirit!'' (Lk 23:46; Ps 31:5).

VII

A Call to Hope: God of the Living
And Not of the Dead

The hope called for by the first commandment of God is a *hope in God* and not in us. Then, it gives us the strength not to despair of ourselves. Let us rediscover it with the Psalms (130:1, 4-5):

> Out of the depths I cry to thee, O LORD!/. . . But there is *forgiveness* with thee. . . ./ I wait for the LORD, my soul waits,/ and in his word I hope;/ my soul waits for the LORD / more than watchmen for the morning. . . .

The first anchorage of hope is the forgiveness of God, Sun of Justice, who will rise up above our darkness.

> Be gracious to me, O God,/ for men trample upon me;/ all day long foemen oppress me,/ my enemies trample upon me all day long,/ for many fight against me proudly./ When I am afraid,/ I put my trust in thee. . . ./ *In God I trust* without fear./ What can flesh do to me? . . ./ They watch my steps./ As they have waited for my life. . . ./ Thou hast kept count of my tossings;/ put thou my tears in thy 'bottle! . . ./ God is for me. . . ./ In God, whose word I praise,/ in the LORD, whose word I praise,/ in God I trust without a fear. . . ./ Thou hast delivered my soul from death,/ yea, my feet from falling,/ that I may walk before God/ *in the light of life.* (Ps 56)

We can say this prayer of the Psalmist with Christ, who lived it, he alone fully — the abandonment of His Passion. True hope consists in trusting in God that at the crucifying crossing of our anguish God Himself wants to give us life.

* * *

The Apostle St. Paul in his letter to Titus (2:11-14) helps us to understand further what the Lord expects from us when he asks us to hope in Him, thus recognizing Him as our God:

> The grace of God has appeared for the salvation of all men,

training us to renounce irreligion and worldly passions and to live sober, upright and godly lives, *awaiting our blessed hope*, the appearing of the glory of our great God and Savior Jesus Christ, who gave himself for us.

The blessed hope, the advent of Jesus Christ our Lord, is the coming of the kingdom of God, life eternal, promised before all the centuries. It is *the resurrection of the dead* and communion with God. Hope that goes beyond all feeling, all imagination, but which pulls man out of the deepest despair, the unanswered fear of nothingness.

Christian hope in its most solid foundation, the promise of God: By the power of the Father, in His risen Son, our whole life will be in the Holy Spirit, torn from the ruin of death and transfigured in the glory of God.

* * *

If the Father of the heavens asks us to hope in Him, what does He do for us who agree to this hope? Indeed, you remember, through his commandments God invites us to act as He acts.

God raised His only Son from the dead. He promises us *a participation in that resurrection*, thereby taking part in eternal life. The prophecy of Isaiah (25:6-9) will be accomplished:

On this mountain the LORD of hosts will make for all peoples a feast. . . . And he will destroy on this mountain the covering that is cast over all peoples, the veil that is spread over all nations. He will swallow up death for ever, and the LORD God will wipe away tears from all faces. . . . It will be said on that day, "Lo, this is our God; we have waited for him that he might save us."

This profession of hope is repeated by John, the seer of Patmos:

"God will wipe away every tear from their eyes. . . . They shall be his people, and God himself will be with them" (Rv 7:17, 21:3).

The joy of being in communion with the life of God, the "blessed hope," is from this moment a reality in our mortal flesh, in which the sacraments of the Church imbue us.

The wine of the eternal wedding feast runs over our lips at the time of the eucharistic feast. The charism of the feast for a royal and priestly people clothes us anew at the time of our baptism.

Love persuades us to hope in God, for we believe, as Jesus said it, that God is " 'the God of Abraham, and the God of Isaac, and the God of Jacob.' He is not God of the dead, but of the living" (Mk 12:26-27).

'You Shall Not Have False Gods'*

Rooted in the Old Testament.
Witness to the New Testament.
Critic and observer of modern times.
Thus does Cardinal Lustiger speak in addressing what at a glance appears to be a remote topic about false gods. In his words, the topic becomes both relevant and inspirational. These sermons, originally heard over Radio Notre-Dame over an eight-week period, retain their freshness and vitality. Their logic is far from labored and their arguments are hardly academic. The sermons say to his listeners: If you believe in the Living God, in the Father, Son, and Holy Spirit, here's what that believing signifies.

In particular, these sermons reflect Cardinal Lustiger's closeness to the New and Old Testaments, taking listener and reader back to Biblical sources and references. It is the Bible read in the light of faith and spoken with the urgency of Christian Witness.

---

*Sermons broadcast on Radio Notre-Dame from October 30 to December 18, 1985. Translated by Jean-Denis Marzi, Ph.D.

I

Idolatry: Adultery?

To answer the question on what is the greatest commandment (Mk 12:28 ff), Jesus compares the commandments concerning God with those concerning one's neighbor.

"Hear, O Israel . . . you shall love the LORD your God with all your heart" (Dt 6:4-5).

"You shall love your neighbor as yourself" (Lv 19:18).

In a very clear manner, biblical tradition has always joined these two commandments into two Tablets of the Law. Thus the First Commandment: "I am the LORD your God, who brought you out of the land of Egypt. . . . You shall have no other gods before me" (Ex 20:2-3). And the Sixth Commandment: "You shall not kill"(Ex 20:13).

God reveals Himself as absolute master of life. Not only does He not sin, but He constantly brings man to life despite his sin. Man, invited to recognize God through faith, hope, and charity, enters into a unique relation of love with God. At the same time, man is able to act toward his neighbor as a substitute for God—who gives life and therefore does not kill — and forgives his neighbor.

In the same way, this clarifies the Second and the Sixth Commandments: "You shall make for yourself no idols. . . ." (Lev 26:1). "I the LORD your God, am a jealous God. . ." (Ex 20:4-6). "You shall not commit adultery" (Ex 20, 14).

Idolatry is adultery and vice versa. The Bible shows it constantly. When the Chosen People worship an idol in place of the living God, God calls them "adulterers" (Jer 9:2). Fidelity to God is compared with conjugal fidelity (note particularly the prophet Isaiah): Israel is the fallen spouse who has prostituted herself and whom God restores to her initial splendor.

Jesus even calls Himself a Bridegroom: "Can the wedding guests mourn as long as the bridegroom is with them? The days will come when the bridegroom is taken away from them, and then they will fast'' (Mt 9:15). Remember also the parable of the wedding feast of the king's son (Mt 22:1 ff). The wedding feast of Cana announces the time of the wedding between God and his people that is ushered in by the coming of the Christ-Messiah into the world.

If the relationship between man and woman illustrates the relationship of God's People toward Him, the illustration must also cast light on the man-woman relationship. Rather than be reduced to a simple act of reproduction between two persons, far from isolating sexuality as if it arises from a biological understanding of the body, human love finds a true place with all its components: its moral demands find their true meaning in the light of God. The relationship encompasses all of man created in God's image and called to imitate God.

Thus by the double enlightenment of the Second and Sixth Commandments, we see how the relationship between men and women can illustrate the relationship between God and humanity. That is why marriage is a sacrament, sign of the union of Christ and His Church: "This is a great mystery, and I mean in reference to Christ and the church." (Eph 5:32).

Idolatry, adultery: they are the same. St. Paul told the Christians at Corinth: "Do not be deceived: neither the immoral, nor idolaters, nor adulterers . . . will inherit the kingdom of God" (1 Cor 6:9-11).

II

God in Man's Image

"You shall not make for yourself a graven image, or any likeness of anything that is in heaven above, or that is in the earth beneath, or that is in the water under the earth; you shall not bow down to them or serve them" (Ex 20:4-5) In front of the One True God, we immediately supersede the idols of the gods of pagan or non-christian religions. This Second Commandment is crucial in the eyes of God: "You shall not do it."

Idols are the work of man. From the moment he lives, sees, and feels, man creates an absolute image although he is created in God's image — God whose name cannot be uttered, who introduces himself: "It is I, your Lord, your God, who has set you free from slavery."

While man finds his greatness and his liberty in turning toward God, Father and Creator, he will become lost if he renounces the living God, chooses whatever he sees, and says, "You are my god." He then cuts himself off from the One who is responsible for his existence. It is the sin of idolatry which traps man in the relationship he creates for himself.

Who are those idols?

First: cosmic forces. The Book of Wisdom describes clearly man's thought process: "[Men did not] recognize the craftsman while paying heed to his works; but they supposed fire, wind, water, and the cycle of the season that man has taken for a god" (Wis 13:1-2).

Truly, the world is the language of God, created by His Word. But man, fascinated by the world's splendor, does not see it as reflecting the divine, nor docs he understand his own intelligence as God's creation. He turns away from the Creator in order to seize a part of creation and to substitute it for God. St. Paul reminds the Christians of Rome: "Ever since the creation of the world, his [God's] invisible nature, namely his eternal power and deity, has been clearly perceived in the things that have been made . . . . but they [men] . . . exchanged the glory of the immortal God for images resembling mortal man or birds or animals or reptiles" (Rom 1:20-23).

Idols can also be an idealized representation of man who adores himself: a projection of man's conscience. The Book of Wisdom expresses this with a cruel clarity (Sg 14:12-21).

Why does God command man not to make idols? The Bible has two answers:

1. Idols are nothing, a piece of wood, says Isaiah, criticizing "all who make idols" as "nothing" (Is 44:9). "Then it [the wood] becomes fuel for man. . . . Half of it he burns in the fire . . . he roasts meat . . . also he warms himself. . . . And the rest of it he makes into a god, his idol; and falls down to it and worships it; he prays to it and says, 'Deliver me, for thou art my god.' " (Is 44:15-17). Far from saving man, this leads him into death.

2. Idols are a mask for the Devil. To love and serve God forces us, in effect, to come out of ourselves, to enter a love which makes us live but also crucifies us, for we are sinners. Whereas the idol — always fashioned after man's desire — gives the illusion of ease. The Devil subtly offers man an image of his desire, whose prisoner he becomes, just as Narcissus was enslaved by his image in the pool.

Christ, from the time of His combat against temptation in the desert until His Passion, illustrates this test of the human heart and shows the double sword of idolatry: enslavement to idols and renunciation of the living God.

The gods created by man can possess splendor and beauty because they reflect man's desire for a sacred manifestation of that part of God which is found in themselves. But these gods are *not* God. God can only be discerned when and only if God reveals Himself to man.

III

Temptations and Struggles

In order to free himself from idolatry and its prison, man must follow the struggle which Christ experienced in his Passion. Man must participate in the mystery of the Cross. We may understand this in the light of the New Testament.

"No one can serve two masters," says Jesus (Mt 6:24), "for either he will hate the one and love the other, or he will be devoted to the one and despise the other. You cannot serve God and mammon." This mammon, money, is an idol. When questioned what was due Caesar (Mt 22:17ff) and when shown a piece of money bearing the Emperor's image, He asked, "Whose likeness and inscription is this?" Doesn't this illustrate a supreme idolatry when man substitutes himself for God as a figure of power?

We find proof in the third temptation of Christ according to Matthew (4:9-10). "All of these," said the Devil, showing Him all the kingdoms of the world in their glory, "I will give you, if you will fall down and worship me." Jesus, nourished by the words of Deuteronomy (6:13), cried out, "Get back, Satan! for it is written 'You shall worship the Lord your God and him only will you serve.'" Here we see refusal of idolatry.

Another form of idolatry can be found in man's heart: the desire to possess the world even though the Lord of the world is God. Christ, stripped of all possessions, King of Glory ridiculed, crowned with thorns, scepter in his hands, bears the sins of man who has become obsessed with power. St. Paul even goes so far as to say: "Their god is the belly" (Phil 3:19). By this he means all of man's biological needs. These needs enslave man in so many ways. Even the senses are substituted in place of God. Man becomes a prisoner of what he desires and makes himself a god.

There is another delicate point heavy with consequences for our

Christian condition today: modern atheism. Is it not exasperating to see the sublimation of desire in our idolatrous civilization, the disillusionment?

This is a harsh reality. Nothing else now exists that our desire has not created and that we do not now confuse with God. Ignoring the Bible, modern man concludes, "There is no God" (Ps 14:1).

Yet it is not too late to discover the true and living God, "showing steadfast love to thousands of those who love me and keep my commandments" (Ex 20:6).

We live in a civilization with unsuspected riches. Our senses and our minds are bombarded by media, by possibilities of communication which serve freedom. Yet they subtly turn on us and enslave us. Thus does television keep us riveted to the screen.

This calls to mind St. Bernard of Clairvaux, the great religious founder. Poet and lover of nature, he would walk in the forest with his eyes closed in order to purify his gaze and to safeguard his spiritual liberty.

What has been fabricated has been substituted for the universe of St. Bernard. Walls and buildings speak. What does a skyscraper say to us? It speaks of admirable technology and of man's reason, but also of a desire for power.

Under these conditions, not to create idols for our ourselves is to retain our liberty of seeing, feeling, and thinking. It is to acquire greater perception, greater insight into what is essential, and to reunite ourselves with God, our Father and our Creator.

IV

The Lamp of the Body (Mt 6:22)

We who today have the most advanced technology at our disposal believe that we are superior to the naive primitives who create idols based on the world they perceive, idols which are projections of their fears, hopes, and ideals. However, more or less consciously we allow ourselves to be drugged by our own products — a deadly drug in the long run.

We make these products our masters, and we are their slaves. In effect, our civilization saturates our minds with images and sounds (enough to burst our eardrums). We are fascinated, and all our senses, notably our sexual desires, become manipulated. Far from being immune to all this, we have become animals of sensation.

Yet, to be really oneself, to hold on to what one believes, to discern what one wishes, it is necessary to concentrate our minds and all our being. We find it perfectly normal that a tennis player concentrate totally on his game to avoid distractions. Should it not be the same for prayer? After all the stimuli we receive, provoking greed, sensuality, vanity, are we not like Pavlovian dogs, are we not like the bull in the arena, stabbed by so many banderillas? How can we strive to control our desires and once again find the truth and peace of God's presence?

To be true to God's Second Commandment demands much hard work from each person — "a guarding of the senses". This rings out like two harmonies in the words of Christ: "The eye is the lamp of the body. So, if your eye is sound, your whole body will be full of light" (Mt 6:22). The eye enables us to see the light which comes from God. It is the light of faith which illuminates and transforms all our sensory existence, the totality of our human condition.

Hence the inescapable admonition: "If your right eye causes you to sin, pluck it out..." (Mt 5:29). Our Lord and Savior thus invites us, not to radical mutilation, but to a radical choice.

Here are two examples of modern idolatry:

If you want to have an open heart toward the love of God and of man, you must learn to be sensitive to the misery of your brothers without a sentimentality which passes as easily as it comes. If you are constantly motivated by the desire to possess things, by the fear of losing out, by the experience of consuming, how can you have the courage to give with an open heart and not in bad faith?

If, despite ourselves, our eyes, ears, and senses are invaded by obsessive desire, our sexuality is no longer free but a stranger to love and it loses its highest spiritual significance, namely that it is the sign of God's love for humanity.

In these two examples, we have destroyed the fundamental balance in human beings. We have profaned a whole part of our existence by removing its divine aspect. From such a point on, we are incapable of understanding God's law in all its depth, richness, and demands as the source of freedom.

And why are we no longer able to understand — for which the young criticize us? Because we have let our hearts, senses, and minds become enslaved by the idols inside us.

Recovering and maintaining this freedom is a matter of self-control, certainly, but also of deliverance. We must pay the price — and this is of primary importance. That means fasting, poverty, forgiveness, and prayer, which now and always coalesce in the struggle alongside Christ, our Liberator.

V

Jesus Christ, Image
of the Invisible God

A particular interpretation of the Second Commandment triggered a crisis in the Eastern Church in the eighth century. Was it legitimate to create images of Christ, the Blessed Mother, and the saints? The Second Ecumenical Council at Nicea (787) addressed the dilemma in this positive way: "Whoever venerates an image venerates the reality which is represented in this image" (*Catholic Faith*, No. 511-512).

The expression of Faith and Christian sensitivity requires figurative images. But in what context?

The invisible God, "whom no man has ever seen or can see" (1 Tm 6:16; cf. also Jn 4:12), Our Lord allows us to see, to touch, and to listen to Him in the form of Christ, the Eternal Word made man. "No one has ever seen God; the only Son who is in the bosom of the Father, he has made him known" (Jn 1:18).

For Jesus is "the image of the invisible God," as St. Paul reminded the Christians from Colossae (1:15). St John adds: "That ... which we have heard, which we have seen with our eyes, which we have looked upon and touched with our hands, concerning the Word of Life ... we proclaim also to you" (1 Jn 1:1-2). This is the witness rendered by the apostles and their generation alone. Jesus is henceforth hidden in God (Col 3:3), and we want to show what has happened by creating statues, pictures, theoretical pieces, films, etc.

But we have with us the effective presence of Him who is the "likeness of God" (2 Cor 4:4). Jesus Christ constantly allows us to glimpse at this image in the sacraments.

Christ's Passion, His death, and His Resurrection are given to us in Baptism, in Confirmation, and during Communion in the Eucharist. We join His struggle, His suffering, and His offering of His life for the salvation of the world in the Sacrament of Anointing. The invitation of the husband to his bride in the Sacrament of

Matrimony is a sign of God's wedding with humanity and Christ's wedding with the Church. Finally, apostolic certitude that He is here, present in the midst of those gathered in His Name, is given to us in the Sacrament of Holy Orders.

This sacramental reality makes the Church an acting image of Christ, an image of the invisible God. To contemplate and to follow Jesus in the sacraments is to enter into His love and to be delivered from idols.

Whoever becomes similar to Christ, loving Him and following Him into His Passion, becomes at the same time an image of Christ, image of His Father. The Church recognizes this by canonizing saints.

Thus, celebrating the sacraments of the Church and recognizing sainthood are the basis and legitimation of "images." We should not confuse these with idols. That is why the images of the saints, the Blessed Mother, and Christ cannot be images like the others. Icons "serve the divine liturgy," say our friends from the Orient. This drives the artist to a deeper exploration of his figures.

Such an aesthetic adventure is a spiritual one. The sacramentality of the Church demands a transcendence in the aesthetic. Why is there such mediocrity in spiritual representations? Is it is not because there is a spiritual crisis in society in which artists play a part? Is there not also a crisis in people's faith? Sooner or later, society reveals its beauty. If we are lacking such beauty in society, it is that the community has not allowed the Light to shine in it.

All images, all things that we can represent are the means for referring to the Supreme Icon, Christ present in His Sacraments, living and concrete images of His actions here and now since He has "dwelt among us" (Jn 1:14).

VI

The Son of God,
Messiah and Servant

Jesus referred to Himself and the Second Commandment in the temptation in the desert. He also did so during Peter's profession of faith at Caesarea Philippi (Mt 16:13ff). The proclamation of his nature as Messiah through the mouth of Simon, son of Jonah, states: "You are the Christ, the Son of the Living God." Jesus received it as the word of His Father who alone was able to reveal it to this apostle. At the same time, He receives Peter as the first stone of the spiritual temple made of living stones, (1 Pet 2:5) of which He is the cornerstone, high priest as well as sacrifice. And he promises His Church, by the power of His Resurrection, victory over death.

But when Christ announces His Passion and His death (Mt 16:21ff), Peter is horrified: "God forbid, Lord! This shall never happen to you!" Jesus, angered, answers harshly, "Get behind me Satan," decrying the idolatrous temptation to use the title of Messiah to avoid rendering to God what is God's. "You are a hindrance for me; for you are not on the side of God but of men."

There is a temptation to substitute human understanding for what God wanted Peter to comprehend about the vocation of the Son of God and about what the Holy Spirit gave to Jesus to accomplish in His humanity, namely as suffering Servant offering brother humans salvation and the love of His Father. There is also the temptation to make the Church something else than the Temple of the Spirit, born from the pierced side of Christ on the Cross (Jn 19:34).

The face of the tempter hides behind the idolatrous temptation. Death also hides there. In the pagan country of Gadarenes, Jesus freed two lunatics from the demons (Mt 8:28ff). Coming out of the tombs, they begin to cry out, "What have you to do with us, O Son of God?" Christ has unmasked death, which holds man, stealing his reason and his freedom.

The Son of God made man teaches us not to be a prisoner of idols:

"Do not be like them [the pagans]. . . . Your father knows what you need" (Mt 6:7-8). Jesus manifests a royal freedom and puts man faced with worry and absolutes of his making on the path of truth in contact with all He has created. Creation is neither a mysterious force which must be conjured up nor is it the mirror of human passions, but a gift of God made for humanity, illuminated by knowledge of the Creator so that man might profit from it and be joyful with his brothers.

"Love your enemies and pray for those who persecute you, so that you may be sons of your Father who is in heaven; for he makes his sun rise on the evil and on the good, and sends rain on the just and unjust" (Mt 5:44-45). Jesus places men in relationship to one another so that none can pretend to be an idol. "The kings of the Gentiles exercise lordship over them, and those in authority over them are called benefactors. But not so with you" (Lk 22:25-26). Christ leads us toward our true vocation as servants of God. By calling upon us to be sons and therefore free—as he tells Peter when reminding him of the taxes for the Temple (cf. Mt 17:26) — God makes brothers of us and leads us toward mutual truth.

Our time has developed a surprising amount of idolatry: horoscopes and the most varied superstition. As far as idols are concerned, especially around Christmastime, we become prisoners of our desire for possession!

Even the divine Infant born in the manger is placed in shop windows and surrounded by such sinful temptations! It is He, the Word of Life, the Image of the Invisible God, who allows us to receive our freedom from God the Father.

"You shall not make for yourself graven images," for you are given "power to become children of God" (Jn 1:12). Yes, Noël: "Grace . . . he manifested . . . through the appearing of our Savior Christ Jesus" (2 Tm 1:10).

VII

The Jealous — Saving — Love of the Father

What does God our Father reveal to us in the Second Commandment?

God reveals himself as "jealous" (Ex 20:5, Dt 6:15), "whose name is Jealous" (Ex 34:14). Joshua at Sichem explains this to the people of Israel, whom he advises to "choose this day" between what is alien and what is our Lord for "he is a holy God; he is a jealous God" (Jos 24:19). God complains about His sons and daughters who have abandoned Him: "They have stirred me to jealousy with what is not god" (Dt 32:21), that is to say, an idol.

Idolatry, as you know, is prostitution, a perversion of love, a negation of love through its caricature. Man, by raising up idols, adores but a reflection of the divine that he sees in the cosmos. Or even more, he adores himself, fascinated by what is divine in him and what has been "created in his own image" (Gn 1:27). Thus, instead of entering into communication and in relationship with God, man cuts himself off from our Lord. Trapped by a divine image of himself and tempted by idols, man ends up in the ultimate blasphemy: "There is no God" (Ps 14:1).

How does God act?

THE CREATOR

The eternal Father, by the sovereign act of His creation, continues to maintain man as a being of flesh and blood whom He created in the image of His Son to be responsible to Him. Freely, He gives us our freedom; lovingly, He gives us the capacity to love; wisely, He gives us intelligence so that we may know Him. He who is Life gives us the means to live.

The act by which man adores God, living and true, is a magnificent example of man's freedom illustrated at its very source.

80

Man, often forgetful by his very nature, becomes truly man in this very act of adoration, for he does not take himself for God, but recognizes that God alone is truly our Lord.

THE REDEEMER

God does not abandon His creation when, in throes of sin, it turns away from the Father, no longer acts as the Son, and disobeys the Holy Spirit. God sends us the eternal Word, which reveals our human condition and dwells among us.

By His Son incarnate with Him and in Him, humanity which has been lost becomes fully filial in the living Temple of God. Humanity can now adore God, pay Him homage, and observe His Commandments. Free as sons. Far from becoming slaves, humans achieve freedom not through fear but through filial love. They take on themselves the will of the Father and grasp what our Lord expects of them.

All the children of God are equal before their Father in heaven. Christ demonstrates this in the Parable of the Prodigal Son: "Son . . . all that is mine is yours" (Lk 15:31). And at the Last Supper (cf. Jn 15-17), Jesus underscores this in His prayer to the Father: "All mine are thine, and thine are mine" (Jn 17:10).

Fulfillment of the Second Commandment in a humanity which has become the people of Christ — and therefore entirely devoted to the Father — becomes an act of adoration and a rejection of the idols which distort and destroy man enslaved by his desires.

God does not envy idols, nor does He compete with them. It is man who places them on the same level, misunderstanding God's love, which is the only measure of man's love. God's is a jealous love, for it alone allows man to live. Only God, who is the sole source of love and freedom, can provide what is love and freedom for man.

"Destined . . . in love to be sons of Jesus Christ" — we are called by the Father to "sing the praise of his glorious grace which he feely bestowed on us in the Beloved" (Eph 1:5-6).

VIII

The Cult of the Spirit
and the Temple of God

Jesus Himself directs us toward total adoration free from all idolatry, adoration which God expects from us. He said to the woman from Samaria: "The hour is coming, and now is, when all the true worshipers will worship the Father in spirit and truth. God is spirit, and those who worship Him must worship in spirit and truth" (Jn 4:23-24).

It is the Holy Spirit who since Pentecost asks us to know the Son and to adore the Father. St. Paul reminds the new Christians from Corinth (1 Cor 12:2-3): "When you were heathen, you were led astray to dumb idols. . . . No one can say 'Jesus is Lord' except by the Holy Spirit" (cf. also 1 Jn 4:2).

It is the Holy Spirit who leads us in worship of the Son, the only true worshiper of the Father. It is the Holy Spirit who makes us adoptive sons capable of crying out, "Abba! Father!" (Rom 8:15ff).

In the face of the temptation to idolatry, God through the Holy Spirit transforms the condition of man and of the Church so that an authentic cult of worship has been created for God the Father through His Son. The Apostle Paul illustrates this Christian and ecclesiastical vocation: "Do you not know that you are God's Temple [the holy of holies] and that God's Spirit dwells in you? . . . For God's temple is holy, and that temple you are" (1 Cor 3:16-17; cf. also 6:19).

"Christ Jesus" himself the cornerstone, in whom the whole structure is joined together and grows into a holy temple in the Lord; in whom you also are built into it for a dwelling place of God in the Holy Spirit (Eph 2:20-22).

St. Peter adds: "Like living stones, be yourselves built into a spiritual house to be a holy priesthood, to offer spiritual sacrifices acceptable to God through Jesus Christ" (1 Pt 2:5).

Assembled in the Synod, we have reaffirmed that the Church is primarily a communion of love, which guards us against the subtle temptation of idolatry in viewing the Church. The exclusive use of the expression "People of God" may be a manifestation of this. In effect, God gave birth to His people by making them His choice. He gave them His covenant.

It is here in the wilderness that people born of God want to become their own master. Created by God, man wants to create his own god: he creates golden calves, gods in the image of his desire. We are tempted in the same way when we make the Church our "possession," tearing it from God who is its Creator.

Father Yves Congar has shown forcefully that the Church was born from the Trinity. It can be readily named "People of God" the Father, because it is the "Body of Christ" and the "Temple of the Holy Spirit." This is presented magnificently in the first chapter of the Vatican II Constitution *Lumen Gentium*.

The eldest son, Israel, by the grace of being the first chosen, attained the dignity of the People of God by becoming the Body of Christ. Cast into death, reborn through the Resurrection, they constitute the Temple of the Spirit prophesied by Ezekiel, announced by the Word made man, whose foundation stone was given to Christ in the person of the Apostle Peter.

That is why the Church can and must offer spiritual sacrifice in complete fidelity to Christ, saying with Him: "Sacrifices and offerings thou hast not desired, but a body hast thou prepared for me. ... I have come to do thy will, O God" (Heb 10:5-7).

St. Paul also writes to the Romans (12:1): "I appeal to you ... to present your bodies as a living sacrifice, holy and acceptable to God, which is your spiritual worship." This truly captures the essence of *Lumen Gentium* (34):

Wanting to pursue equally, by means of the laity, His witness and His service, Jesus Christ supreme and eternal priest, brings life to them through the Holy Spirit, and pushes them unremittingly toward total good and total perfection.

For those who join themselves intimately to His life and to His mission, he bestows, in addition, a portion of his sacerdotal charge for the exercise of a spiritual cult in view of the glorification of God and the salvation of men. That is why the laity receive, by virtue of their consecration though Christ and the blessing of the Holy Spirit, the admirable vocation and the means which allow the Holy Spirit to produce in them more and more abundant fruit. In effect, all their activities and their apostolic enterprises, their familial and conjugal life, their daily labors, their spiritual and physical activities, if they are carried out in the Spirit of God, even life's trials as long as they are patiently endured, all these become "spiritual sacrifices," pleasing to God, through Jesus Christ (1 Peter 2, 5); and in the Eucharistic celebration, these offerings are joined with the sacrifice of the Body of Our Lord to be offered in complete piety to the Father. It is in this way that the laity consecrate the entire world to God, giving to God everywhere by the sanctity of their life, a cult of adoration.

PART II

REJOICE
IN CHRISTIANITY

On the day before Easter in 1984, Cardinal Lustiger rejoiced in the "Call of Christ" before an assembly of young and old who were about to be baptized. After proclaiming that the "mystery of the Resurrection bursts forth in the liturgy of baptism," he welcomed them, fellow Christians, as proof of Christ's love. In a memorable passage, he described what they have "glimpsed" and their calling:

"You have glimpsed that it is beautiful, in a man or woman's life, to become a disciple of Christ and to live with the love of God, the Spirit of God in one's heart. You have glimpsed that it is possible to dare to overcome one's weakness, to hope to live according to the law of love of Jesus Christ. You hope that this is not only a needful possibility but an assured reality. You are called to be, in this aged world, the ferment of a new world; in this sick world, the sign of healing."

The conclusion captures the spirit of rejoicing in Christianity that permeates this second section of his sermons and interviews:

"The fruitfulness and the beauty of a life following Christ surpasses all that one can imagine. God does not fool us. He keeps his word a hundredfold, far beyond what we imagine. Do not fear. You are loved and you are called to become the witnesses of Love."

When Christ Says to Us: 'I Am the Way, the Truth, and the Life'*
(Jn 14:1-12)

Christians, take heed. Here is stirring affirmation of the challenge and promise of Christianity.

This Sunday sermon, delivered in the Cathedral of Notre Dame during the Christian affirmation of Eastertime (in 1987), makes it clear that Christians do not ask what Christianity can do for them. Instead, they want to know what they can do to respond to Christ, his example, his message, his mission.

Cardinal Lustiger sets forth the message and the mission of Christianity with an assurance that challenges the lukewarm and the wavering. At the same time, he rejects self-centered, narrow-minded excess that undermines the universality he proclaims in Christianity. He refuses, as he emphasizes, to let either skepticism or fanaticism get in the way of the Christian mission.

What comes through is the voice of passionate reasonableness, the words of a man who has discovered Christ and, cherishing the discovery, exults in proclaiming it.

---

*Translated by Rebecca H. Balinski.

The Way, the Truth, the Life

If we stop to consider the tremendous import of Jesus's assertion that He is "the way, and the truth, and the life," we might be tempted to reject it. Have we not, after all, discovered the relativity of humanity's beliefs and religious convictions? We know full well that the assertion has been rejected by a great many of our contemporaries who, after leaving the confined world of their upbringing, have encountered other cultures, other civilizations, other spiritual "ways" from East to West. They have asked themselves: "Aren't Jesus' words the source of an untenable claim by a rather arrogant group of people who profess their faith in Christ as an absolute? Should his words not be interpreted from the perspective of relativism? Should we not admit that other peoples find equivalent words in other religions?" Such are the doubts that can assail a person whose eyes have been opened on our world.

At the other extreme, there can arise the frightening and constantly recurring caricature of diverse people who lay hold of Christianity and even the adjective "Catholic" and claim them as their exclusive property. They reduce the religion of Christ to the expression of their own sacredness. Thinking that their national or ethnic identity is venerable, they put the cross of Christ in the service of self-worship — indeed, in the service of their will to dominate.

What a horrifying caricature of "election," of God's gratuitous choice of a man, a people, of Christ, and of His Church! No human group can ever claim to monopolize Christ. When He reveals that He is "the way, and the truth, and the life," it is because He is urging us to participate in his divine condition as Redeemer of all mankind.

It is Christ, and Christ alone, who designates His Church and His people; it is Christ who traces the mark of recognition on those who have received the mission to be the presence and the sign of love in this world. When man's pride attempts to appropriate Christ, God made man, to make Him an object of worship for a specific society or national group, the Church becomes a captive.

On this subject, the Pope has often recalled certain misadventures in the West.

During a recent pastoral visit to Germany, he evoked with courageous Christian lucidity — what a lesson for all of us! — the terrible apostasy of misappropriating faith in Jesus Christ and even words from Scripture and the meaning of election in order to subjugate them to a national ambition, a race, a "blood." When soldiers wore belt buckles with the inscription "Gott mit uns," it was a blasphemy as idolatrous as all the blasphemies which make the author of Revelation tremble before the Beast who clothes himself in God's signs in order to usurp His divine power.

O Catholics, my brothers and sisters, beware of assuming that this temptation has been removed forever!

In short, when Christ is presented as an absolute, we can feel troubled and hesitant. To skeptics, Christianity appears to be simply one among other religious experiences; or else, there are people whose will to dominate reduces faith in Christ to a cultural or national identity.

Are our Christian societies doomed to oscillate between skepticism and fanaticism, between a belief in the relativity of the Christian faith and its entirely human and ethnic assertion?

What, then, can Christ's assertion mean today for those of us who live in societies frequently rootless and characterized by so much contradictions and hatred?

Listen carefully to His words. Jesus was speaking to His apostles on the eve of His Passion, but the words are also spoken to us today in the Church by the resurrected Christ, spoken to those of us who are His members, His Church.

"Let not your hearts be troubled; believe in God, believe also in me."

Christ's call places all of His disciples in a very well defined position, because the One who is gathering us together is Christ Himself. Whatever our skin color, our racial or national origin, He is calling us to follow Him.

"Believe in God, believe also in me" — it is an astonishing, almost intolerable statement. God alone can ask faith of man—that is, the unconditional turning over of his freedom, his intelligence, his love to the One who is their source. But this total submission, unlike all others, is not enslaving, because God alone is God. Believing in Christ with the same faith due to God is recognizing that Jesus is "the Way," the only Way toward the heavenly Father. We are not putting our faith in a leader, a country, an ideology, or a cause. Our faith is in God, who alone can ask such adherence of us.

"In my Father's house are many rooms; if it were not so, would I have told you that I go to prepare a place for you? And when I go to prepare a place for you, I will come again and will take you to myself, that where I am you may be also."

Jesus says, "my Father's house." That means God's Temple, the Temple where God reveals Himself, the Holy of holies where divine Glory resides. To conceive of Israel as recipient of God's presence in its Temple is already a great challenge to human intelligence. Speaking of the heavenly Temple, Jesus is now saying that He is going to have access to this holy Place, presenting Himself as the high priest who alone has the right to enter there.

And He adds, ". . . that where I am you may be also." In other words, He is designating us as a priestly people since He is proposing, as a promise and a hope, that we enter along with him into the celestial sanctuary, into the Holy of holies where God has established His Glory. Jesus is asking us to place ourselves in His hands, so that He can take us with Him and give us access to the Holy of holies, to His Father.

"And you know the way I am going."

These enigmatic words refer to the "way" of His Passion. For Jesus to concentrate all possibilities of access to the mystery of God in His Passion shocks human intelligence even more than He challenges Israel's faith by declaring that He is the Messiah, the Son of God.

Jesus makes His cross the obligatory point of passage toward the heavenly Father. Far from sparing those who follow Him from the suffering the have been hoping to escape, Christ only increases it in a way. And Thomas protests, "Lord, we do not know where you are going; how can we know the way?" And Jesus replies, "I am the way, and the truth, and the life; no one comes to the Father but by me.''

● *Jesus is the Way*, because in His condition as Son of God made man, in His mystery as the humiliated Messiah — crucified and seemingly crushed — He presents Himself as the Mediator through whom all of humanity must pass in order to gain access to God the Father. He is the one in whom men and women must live in order to reach God, since He is the one who has accomplished perfectly the will of His heavenly Father.

● *Jesus is the Truth*: not the truths that man embraces and then rejects, not the coherent arguments that man constructs and then destroys, but Truth itself, which is revealed as Person and situates all of us as persons. In Jesus, God says ''thou'' to us, and we can say ''thee'' to him. Jesus is Truth, the Light of the world and of our individual lives. He is the Truth of our Creator and Redeemer from whom our existence springs, He shows us who we are precisely because knowing who God is means that we are able to discover the truth about ourselves. All the other truths are merely a collection of learning which will perish as all human memories accumulated by man perish. The only immortal memory is the memory of God and our memory in God. All else is a splendid contrivance of human intelligence. Although human intelligence is certainly a sublime instrument of power and beauty, it is a mirage and an evanescent cloud when there does not arise within the world the voice of a person capable of saying ''I'' because God says ''thou'' to him. Moreover, the individual can say ''I'' only because God has united all humanity by addressing us collectively as ''you.''

● *Jesus is life*, because in the relationship implied by the interplay of ''personal'' pronouns the mystery of personal love of God is revealed. Christ is the one who says to us: ''*My* Father and *your* Father.'' He can ask of us the faith which the Father asks of us since it is he who gives us the Life which comes from God, the Life which destroys sin and death.

At this point in the Gospel, as He approaches the moment when His life will be offered, Jesus continues to explain patiently the work being accomplished by the Father who dwells in Him, because He wants to show that by believing in Him, we believe in the Father.

"Believe me that I am in the Father and the Father in me; or else believe me for the sake of the works themselves. Truly, truly, I say to you, he who believes in me will also do the works that I do; and greater works than these will he do because I go to the Father. Whatever you ask in my name, I will do it, that the Father may be glorified in the Son."

The nature of our adherence to Christ is such that the Apostle Peter recalls it by using the same words as those found in Exodus (19:5), designating the People of Israel as the kingdom of priests and a holy nation chosen by God: "But you are a chosen race, a royal priesthood, a holy nation, God's own people, that you may declare the wonderful deeds of him who called you out of darkness into his marvelous light. Once you were no people but now you are God's people; once you had not received mercy but now you have received mercy" (1 Peter 2:9-10).

"A holy nation, God's own people": there is no other glorious title in this affirmation, no other claim to truth in this act of faith except the participation in Christ's sacerdotal mission, obeying "unto death, even death on a cross."

Confessing that Christ is the Way, the Truth, and the Life means daring to believe that we have been engaged by Him in the Spirit, that we are committed to following Him, that the world is not a strange enigma, but that God is at work in human history and in the individual history of every person.

Henceforth, God's plan for the world's salvation includes our individual faces: this is no cause for boasting, it entails no special advantages or immunities: our inclusion in God's work is a grace and a *mission*.

Henceforth, we are marked with the cross of Christ to be the sign and the sacrament of the suffering Messiah for those around us, and to make it possible for those around us to decipher God's work in a world which at times can appear absurd in its contradictions, unbearable in its chaos and anguished cries.

Deciphering both the mystery of the suffering Just One and the hope of glory that His suffering contains can be done — and must be done — only by those who share the condition of the crucified Messiah. This, then, is our mission as Christians.

Yes, we do dare to say that Christ is the Way, the Truth, and the Life and that "no one comes to the Father" but by Him. However, in saying this, we are not excluding any person or claiming any privileges.

Other than that of being crucified with the One who resurrects us.

Other than that of working for increase in love and forgiveness along with the One who loves and has forgiven us.

Other than that of being truly the Church God has chosen to reveal to all men and women, here and now, the hope that endures forever.

Our Lives: The Dwelling of God*

Cardinal Lustiger calls this sermon a "meditation." The passage on which he bases his reflections is the best introduction to what follows:

> *The next day again John was standing with two of his disciples, and he looked at Jesus as he walked, and said, "Behold, the Lamb of God!" The two disciples heard him say this, and they followed Jesus. Jesus turned and saw them following, and said to them, "What do you seek?" And they said to him, "Rabbi" (which means Teacher), "where are you staying?" He said to them, "Come and see." They came and saw where he was staying; and they stayed with him that day, for it was about the tenth hour. One of the two who heard John speak, and followed him, was Andrew, Simon Peter's brother. He first found his brother Simon and said to him, "We have found the Messiah" (which means Christ). He brought him to Jesus.*
>
>

John 1, 35-42

---

*This sermon delivered January 20, 1985, in Notre Dame Cathedral, was translated by Jean-Denis Marzi, Ph.D.

Our Lives: The Dwelling of God

The word of God in John (1:35-42) enables us to appreciate the harmony in the mystery of our salvation:

1. The Church, Temple and Body of Christ;
2. Christ, Himself, the Dwelling of God, and
3. Ourselves, beings created in the image of God, Temples of the Spirit in our mortal bodies.

From the triple mystery of the dwelling of God among men — in the Church, in Christ, in our bodies — we are enlightened as we confront a decisive and inescapable question for our age: What, finally, is man? What is man in his corporal condition?

At this very time when our increased knowledge and great power over human genetics cause that knowledge and power to flounder in darkness, what is human and what is not? At this very time, the gravest questions are posed by the progress of human intelligence in understanding man's appropriate condition. At this very time, divine light cast upon the human condition is necessary in order to save what must be saved of the dignity of man and of his existence.

The Church, Christ, and man in his body are interdependent. I am convinced that the way in which we treat the Church is the sign of the way in which we treat Christ, and the way in which we treat Christ is the test of the way we treat ourselves.

THE CHURCH

Throughout the Old Testament and in the message of Jesus, idea and image are present constantly. Jesus speaks of a living Temple and we constitute its "living stones." Its unity, its plenitude, its assembly are realized by the Holy Spirit who chose us. He gives us not only the coherence of a building, the entity of an assembled body, but makes all of us the living and holy Temple of God.

The Church is that edifice founded on the apostles, the twelve columns of the Church, as the Scripture says (Gal 2:9) and the place where the glory of God is to dwell. Henceforth, no other human edifice will have the same grandeur, the same plenitude, the same history as this new dwelling built by the Holy Spirit.

The three-times-Holy Temple of Jerusalem — where above the Cherubim resides the Glory of God, according to the vision of the prophet Isaiah — and the churches and temples built by man are by definition finished temples. Their perfection reflects a human intelligence which can conceive the edifice only according to its measure.

The fascinating beauty is due in part to the fact that our intelligence finds in its measured enclosure the security of a space which we have constructed, which we can delimit, which is stable, fixed, even if at each step, with each look, we perceive new aspects. What is proper to the Temple which God builds with these living stones of our lives is that no one can make its plan but Him. No one can provide its coherence except the Spirit who dwells there.

Its construction is not finished with historical measurements. New stories are being continually added. To the extent that this edifice is compared with the growth of a body, it draws its perfection from the infinite love of God, who constructs and inhabits it.

Its only measure is the design of Infinite *love*. The splendor of the spiritual temple ''not built by human hands'' — which is the Church — escapes us, whereas an edifice in stone is possessed in its beauty by our eyes, by our hands, by our senses.

CHRIST, THE DWELLING OF GOD

The spiritual Temple, the Church of Christ, comprises not only the people of our planet living today, but also all those innumerable, unknown people who are buried in death and live with Christ. They are more present from the weight of their lives and their love than beings who today walk on this earth and speak with a human voice. Gathered in hope is the immense crowd of men and women whom God loves, calls, and assembles to constitute that Spiritual Temple which is the Church.

So, from the first page of the Gospel according to St. John, the disciples come to live with Christ, Him whose dwelling is the Temple of God, the House of His Father.

The very manner in which we Christians consider this Spiritual Temple, the Church, enables us to be witnesses of a stronger reality:

the Temple, which is the Body of Jesus. According to another image used by Christ, we are His Body. St. John makes us understand this when he records for us, before the Passion, the enigmatic challenge of Jesus before the Temple of Jerusalem: "Destroy this Temple, and in three days, I shall rebuild it" [John 2, 19].

This was a provocative and absurd proposal to the ears of His listeners, incomprehensible for the disciples of whom the evangelist will say in effect: "They understood later that Jesus was talking about the Temple of His Body" — His own Body, which would for the love of us sink into our death in order to give us life. In what way do we adore, do we love this Body, infinitely holy, of the Word of God, which has taken flesh of the Virgin Mary, only Son of God become man, the very mystery of the presence in our humanity, of the God unknown and infinite revealed through His Son?

The Body of Christ, delivered for us our nourishment in the Eucharist, blood poured out for us for the forgiveness of sins so we can drink of the Resurrection and of divine life.

Body of Christ, our brother, son of Adam; Body of Christ, external Word, son of God, by whom we can become children of God! Divine life presents in humanity saves the human condition not only from its mortal weakness, but also from its doom and gives it communion with God, Life eternal.

Yes, as we treat the Church, we treat Christ: infallible test of the truth of our faith regarding Christ. He who despises the Church as the Body of Christ cannot say that he truly believes that the unique body of Jesus, born of the Virgin Mary, is the Body of the Son of God.

The test of faith in Christ, God and man, is our faith in the divine presence of the Spirit in that body of Christ which we form, the Church.

Perhaps you think that we are here inside a narrow circle where faith enlightens only the believer. Perhaps you think that this meditation has meaning only for the disciple of Jesus. Yet these two mysteries — the body of Jesus born of the Virgin Mary and the ecclesiastical body of Christ — point to the Salvation of man in His body.

What salvation? From what do we need to be saved?

I now arrive at the precise point at which I would like to end our meditation.

We must be saved from the scorn of the destruction of man, by man. We must be saved from the refusal toward which we are almost fatally led: to consider the divine greatness of man, of any man. When human reason — a reflection of divine intelligence and a gift of God — is no longer received from God and seeks by itself to master our historical and corporal condition and to understand what a human being is, suddenly it no longer knows what to say. It stumbles!

HUMAN TEMPLES OF THE HOLY SPIRIT

Who is human? Is the embryo human? The old or sick man who can no longer control his movements, is he a human being? Is the enemy a human being? He whom we call savage, is he a human being?

The one we call deviant, is he a human being? The one who is called mad, is he a human being? The one whom all despise because he is called perverse — and, maybe is — is he a human being? Who will decide what is man? Who will decide who is a man?

Why is there more respect for that fragile accumulation of human cells which form an embryo than for any other accumulation of cells from any other living being? How are we going to discuss the matter?

How are we going to legislate? How are we going to understand what respect is owed to man? Who will decide that a particular part of the human species does not deserve a particular unconditional respect?

I do not pretend to step into areas where researchers, jurists, men of all sciences can exercise their knowledge. I speak to you as an apostle of Jesus Christ, witness of God's word, charged with man's salvation.

Do you see what we need to be saved from?

From the *ignorance* which would lead man not to know any longer who he is.

Now, here is the *plus* that we are: The temple of God, each of us, in our corporal condition.

97

"Your body is the temple of the Holy Spirit," says St. Paul [1 Cor 6:9], echoing the words of Jesus. "You must be born anew" [John 3:3], that is to say from God, from the Spirit.

We are the Temple of the Holy Spirit as the Church is the body of Christ, as Christ born of the Virgin Mary is the external Son of God.

Each of us, the most scorned and the most famous, the mightiest and the weakest, the most worthy in the eyes of God and the most unworthy, dying or still in the womb of his mother — in one word, anyone who is part of the human condition — is infinitely sacred as the dwelling of God among men. He must be treated with the same sacred respect we owe our creator and Redeemer. All that is our species is intended to constitute the Temple of God.

Surely, we are sinners, blinded even to homicide — the first sin of Adam's children in Cain's killing of his brother Abel. But the mystery of the Redemption of Christ, who takes away our sins and who on the Cross delivered us and saves us from death, is the fullest measure of the deliverance and salvation God wants to accomplish in us. In Christ, our brothers who are enemies receive the command to love each other.

Thus you understand, my friends, the prophetic importance of this mystery of the Temple of God, ecclesial Body of Christ, He whose flesh is that of the eternal Word and who makes of us the Temples of the Holy Spirit. There is only one God.

As disciples of Christ, we know that man created in the image and likeness of God is called to be the Temple of the Holy Spirit. We know also that we must — with the force of reason, liberty and respect — defend the divine and absolute dignity of any man, of all that is human.

This is not a particular opinion but a universal truth, a certitude which rests on our faith in the love of our Father and Creator, and for that we must "Obey God, rather than men" [Act 5:29]. We must do so with the same fidelity as Jesus, who gave His life for our redemption and for our lives.

Thus human is a word full of hope which today the Church gives us to understand, a word full of force, of beauty, of rigor. That word makes us understand that labor — such as the labor of the woman giving birth — that pain — such as the pain of the Redeemer and the pain of the Lamb of God who takes away the sins of the world — are sources of joy given to us so that we may bear testimony of it to the world.

Joining With Christ
in Spiritual Combat*

Cardinal Lustiger calls the Feast of All Saints a "reminder" of every person's destiny of eternal life and speaks out against shrinking from the hope of becoming a saint. "All those who are baptized have a call to sanctity," he has told one interviewer. "To dare to hope to become a saint is not to be pretentious, but to acknowledge that we are sinners and to believe that God forgives and transforms us. It is enough to let God guide us."

What, then, about temptation and about losing our way? What can Christians learn from the Temptation of Christ? What does it mean to turn away from evil and toward good?

In this series of four sermons broadcast over Radio Notre-Dame in March 1988, Cardinal Lustiger issues a call to join with Christ in "spiritual combat." It is the hard — and unavoidable — road to sanctity and saintliness, a road that everyone must travel.

But not alone, as the message of Christianity proclaims.

---

*Translated by Jean-Denis Marzi, Ph.D.

I

To Fight Against Temptation

Lent reminds us of the urgency of joining with Christ in spiritual combat. But against whom? Against what? In the "Lord's Prayer," we ask: "Lead us not into temptation," or, according to a more subtle translation: "Do not allow us to be led into temptation."

What is at the heart of this combat?

Christ himself lived it. From before His baptism and His forty days in the desert to the hour of His Passion and His "agony" (in other words, His combat) at Gethsemane, during His whole life, Christ was put to the test. At times, His friends tested Him, such as Peter's denial at the hour of His death (Mt 16:23). At times, His various contradictors laid traps for Him, such as the question concerning tribute due to Caesar (Mt 22:15-22).

Spiritual combat consists of fighting back when put to the test or when faced with temptation. In the terminology of the moral life, the word "temptation" defines our attraction toward that which we know to be evil.

Advertising abuses the term to the point of caricature: "Let yourself be tempted by our prices," or "It's so good, it's almost sinful!" We speak of "being drawn to the forbidden fruit," a reference to the second account of creation, where the fruit of the Tree of Knowledge of Good and Evil appeared beautiful and seductive to our first parents.

To fall into temptation means to fall prey to a desire which we know is bad for us, to succumb to it. We do so by our senses with a list of sins that are only too familiar: gluttony, envy, hedonism, etc. Or, by not living up to a moral ideal, whether it be marital fidelity, chastity, honesty, respect for the property of others, respect for others, even reducing ourselves to the point of insulting and hurting someone simply because of the color of his skin!

101

Resisting temptation must become an "art," a "path to follow," a "spiritual training" to separate us from what leads us into evil, guided by a wisdom accumulated through centuries of experience and taught by Scripture itself: "Not to follow after your own heart and your own eyes," the Lord advises Moses (Num 15:39).

To speak of irresistible temptation is to misunderstand the true nature of man. For, aside from drinking, drugs, or extreme physical duress which take away self-control and self-mastery, human beings are superior to all other living creatures by the ability to direct their will, to control their freedom and their emotions, and by their capacity to choose.

As athletes learn to control their muscles, their brains, their hearts and their emotions in order to give total concentration to one task, so can it be in the moral and spiritual realm when faced with temptation. We can, we must control our free will.

To accomplish this, we must distance ourselves from what we know is evil. Knowing our limits and our weaknesses, we must separate ourselves from the fatal mechanisms which lead us to evil acts, as a stone roles down a steep slope. Avoiding occasions of sin is nothing but wisdom. *There* resides true moral responsibility.

In its truest and fundamental sense, to fight temptation is to want to choose good and, therefore, to want to choose God. It is putting one's destiny in God's hands and it is praying. "Rise and pray," says Christ, "that you may not enter into temptation."

At the root of the human condition lies the mystery of evil. "Be sober, be watchful," Peter writes to the first Christians, "Your adversary, the devil, prowls around like a roaring lion, seeking some one to devour. Resist him, firm in your faith" (1 Pt 5:8-9).

The true power which will free us from evil is the power of Christ. Where our weakness enchains us, Our Savior makes us capable of triumph by allowing us to enter into the all-powerful love of God. That is why Paul recommends: "Be strong in the Lord and in the strength of his might. Put on the whole armor of God, that you may be able to stand against the wills of the devil. . . . Pray at all times in the Spirit, with all prayer and supplication" (Eph 6:10-11, 18).

II

Unmasking Evil in the Guise of Good

What does the struggle against temptation consist of? Is it man torn between the righteous path, which he wants to follow, and desire and passion, which his reason can no longer control?

It is more than this. It is stranger still: Man is no longer able to distinguish between what is truly good and what is truly evil. Our conscience, that which enables us to recognize evil, is blinded. This darkness, this blinding of our conscience, is revealed to us by Christ, who is our Deliverer.

Consider Simon and the Fallen Woman (Lk 7:36ff). What is the difference between Simon, a just man, a friend of Christ, and this woman? Are we justified in contrasting the smug conformity of the former with the contrite heart of the latter?

In truth, both are guilty of sin — But, it is only the woman who has fully realized her sin in the pardon that she has received. She prostrates herself at Jesus' feet. However, Simon, does not see in front of Jesus that he, also, is a sinner whom Christ can deliver from evil.

Jesus tries to show us this in three parables.

The Pharisee and the Tax Collector
(Lk 18:9-14)

Both go up to the Temple to pray. The Pharisee makes a list of his good deeds.

The tax collector realizes that he has sinned and humbly begs: God, be merciful to me a sinner." Jesus declares: "This man went down to his house justified rather than the other. . . ." Wherein lies the difference? The Pharisee, blinded by himself, cannot see where his sin lies.

Poor Lazarus and the Rich Man
(Lk 16, 19ff)

The rich man does not see Lazarus covered with ulcers and starving at his doorstep. When they have both died, it is then that he sees Lazarus at Abraham's side and realizes the mistake that he has made. In his torment, the rich man begs Abraham to send Lazarus to warn his five brothers, so that they may avoid that place of Hell. But, Abraham replies: "If they do not listen to Moses or the Prophets, even if they raise the dead, they will not be convinced."

This illustrates the hardening of man's heart under the shell of sin, as well as the blinders of self-righteousness under the truth of God's gaze.

The Good Samaritan
(Lk 10:29-37)

The first two men who pass by the wounded man, the priest and the Levite, have no less humanity than the man who stops. They do not see the wounded man; the Samaritan does. Their conscience is blinded.

Let us listen, now, to the two last companions of Christ: The two criminals crucified at his side. (Lk 23:39-43).

All three are condemned to the same death according to law. One of the criminals begins to insult Jesus: "Are you not the Christ? Save yourself and us." The other condemned man replies: "We indeed [suffer] justly, for we are receiving the due reward of our deeds; but this man has done nothing wrong."

As opposed to the first criminal, the latter, because he sees that he has sinned, instead of insulting Jesus, begs: "Jesus, remember me when you come in your Kingly power." To this Jesus answers: "Truly, I say to you, today you will be with me in Paradise."

Temptation, as we have seen, does not limit itself to the attraction toward evil. When evil is confused with good and presents itself under the "cloak of good," the spiritual struggle demands that we reverse our hearts, our minds and our intelligence. We must work on our conscience. As long as our conscience can uncover evil, man remains free to choose God. But we can succeed only if Christ's power delivers us from our blindness.

On several occasions, Christ foiled the traps laid by His adversaries and uncovered the temptations set by those closest to Him — whenever evil was shrouded under the guise of good. In the example of Peter, after his profession of faith to Cesarea Philippi, he was horrified by the coming of Christ's death and protests: (Mt. 16:21-23): "God forbid, Lord! This shall never happen to you." Peter thought that he was doing good in reacting as a disciple who loves his Master.

But Jesus unmasks the evil in Peter's reaction. It offers the pretext of doing good by responding to Peter's friendship and not risking His life, thereby evading the will of the Father.

III

Accepting the Light
of the Church's Word

Today, our difficulty is not so much giving in to evil, for human beings, basically, are drawn to good, are created to do good. Rather, the problem is pretending to pursue good while choosing evil. This is aggravated when the majority call evil "good," and people "canonize" behavior which has been considered "evil." They call it good. Everyone says it, everyone does it so it must be good.

In actuality, the conscience of such individuals is walled up with falsehood and blindness, as Paul writes to the Romans (1:21): "They went astray in false reasoning and their foolish hearts have fallen prey to darkness."

But the situation is even more serious. Certain people refuse to listen to God's Commandment in the name of conscience. In effect, they say that the authority of the Church is only the subjective opinion of a few priests, at best, authority stemming from the conscience of the Pope or certain bishops. That amounts to denying any objective consistency in the revelation of the will of God. It sets aside the reality of the Incarnation of the Word.

As John states when Jesus speaks to Nicodemus (Jn 3:19-21): "Light has come into the world, and man loved darkness rather than light because their deeds were evil." And, so, it is true: "Everyone who does evil hates the light, and does not come to the light, lest his deeds should be exposed." Let us remember, however, that only Christ, Bearer of the Lord's Word, who was sent into this world that it might be saved, can make such judgement of good and evil.

Those who do evil and will not acknowledge it live in bad faith, refusing that faith capable of saving them. Those who live truthfully come toward the light, so that their works may be seen and accomplished in the name of the Lord.

How, then, can anyone blind his conscience? From concession to concession, weakness to weakness, everyone seeks to justify what he does. The smallest string of weaknesses, the imperceptible list of concessions and the minute accumulation of cheating obstruct any path to the truth. Each individual is responsible for what he has become and must work toward his own salvation.

What can the believer, faced with these obstacles, do?

The first recourse, of course, is to rediscover an attitude of faith and to tell oneself: "I believe that what I am doing is good. I may not understand the situation the Church attests to. But in spite of the judgement of my conscience, I want to believe in God. He is speaking to me today by means of this Church, which He assists through the Holy Spirit."

Fundamentally, the act of faith demands that you do not reduce the Word of the Church to being only the word of a man of the Church, who defends his personal opinion—in other words, merely a spokesman. "For so," said Jesus to his disciples, "men persecuted the prophets who were before you," (Mt 5:12), "stoning those who are sent" (Mt 23:3).

For they meant to kill the word of the prophets, to contest their role as prophet, which is to *speak before* the people on behalf of the Lord.

Those who have received the apostolic mission bear testimony to the truth of God by the force of the Holy Spirit given to the Church. If, that word seems to you incomprehensible or revolting, at least listen with faith and respect. It comes from God. Maintain that spiritual tension between your opinion and the Word of God. There lies the real debate of faith: dialogue and not *self-absorbed* soliloquy.

Pray so that faith works in you, and little by little, enlightens your conscience and transforms your intelligence. Pray that you know your sin. The one who discovers that he is a sinner, or, in which way he is a sinner has made enormous progress in love.

God alone can accomplish the work of purification, of clarification, of conversion in order to cure man of his blindness by giving him Light.

This is the grace we must ask and obtain for one another.

IV

'If You Are the Son of God. . . .'

To surrender to the chaos of evil or to mistake evil for good: Clearly, these two cases of temptation presented previously could not apply to Jesus. The Son of God made man would never prefer His own will to the Will of God or evade the love He must have for His Father and which He has for us, his brothers. His conscience is never blinded.

What, then, is the temptation of Christ told by the Evangelists? What fundamentally is temptation for the Christian?

When God has shown the greatness of His grace, it is not so much to be tempted by evil, but to be tested on the very gifts God has granted us.

Remember the temptation of Christ in the desert (Mt 4:1-11).

"If you are the Son of God," the devil said twice.

Here is the key sentence of the temptation. Jesus knows he is the Son of God. Would the devil like to induce Jesus to doubt it? No, not really. More cunningly, he wants to incite Jesus to seize, as a prey, that state of Son of God (cf Phil 2:6), in order to act instead of God His Father.

"If you are the Son of God, tell those stones to become bread," says the tempter. In other words: "Since you are the Son, act, instead of the Father. Seize the gift you have received and reject the one who gave it to you." Jesus answers by quoting the Scripture, the Word of God: "Man shall not live by bread alone, but by every word that proceeds from the mouth of God."

By quoting Deuteronomy (8:3), Jesus rejects the temptation to make Himself, in His humanity, the source of His own existence. Son of God, perfectly obedient and loving, He is fully aware that He received His life from the Father in Heaven.

The tempter uses the Word of God to provoke Jesus, whom he has transported to the pinnacle of the Temple, above the Holy of Holies, to launch a challenge to God: "He will give his angels charge of you," and "On their hands they will bear you up lest you strike your foot against a stone" (cf. Ps 91:11-12). Jesus repels the tempter by another sentence from Scripture, by the Word of God: "You shall not put the LORD your God to the test," or "You will not tempt the Lord your God" (Dt. 6:16).

Remember, too, Christ on the Cross (Mt 27:38-44). Passersby and soldiers insult Him: "If you are the Son of God, save yourself. If you are the Son...." The scribes, elders, high priest mock him, and brigands insult Him: "He saved others; he cannot save *himself*. He trusts in God; let God deliver him now, if he desires him; for he said, "I am the Son of God.' "

Thus, on the wood of the cross, at the hour when Jesus reaches the end of His mission as Redeemer, at the hour where the eternal Son who shares the glory of the Father takes upon His humanity all our wounds, all our sins — at this hour of His passion, Jesus is tempted about His filial divinity.

However (cf. Phil 2:6-8), Son of God though He was, He wanted to make Himself "obedient unto death" and enter into this emptying of Himself by which He changes the fall and spiritual annihilation of man into a source of pardon and of life.

Thus the temptation of Christ can only be understood in terms of gifts received. For Christ, the gifts received in His humanity are the highest man can receive. That is why the strongest temptations do not occur in the first steps of Christian life.

The more advanced we are in Christian life, the more the test of temptation presents itself as violent and subtle, bearing precisely upon the graces given to us. The more God overwhelms us, the more we have to be watchful of spiritual battle with the evil one.

Therefore, it is not only a matter of resisting temptation and asking God to take it away. For we know our weakness; we stumble if the Lord does not carry up and help us. We must share the combat of Christ against evil and the adversary of man.

This spiritual combat is a sharing in the Passion of Christ and associates us with the triumph of His glorious Cross. Precisely as He promises us: "In the world you have tribulation; but be of good cheer, I have overcome the world" (Jn 16:33).

Toward the Year 2000:
Faith and Courage*

How does the man of faith view today's troubled world and see the way ahead for the believing Christian?

The answer unfolds in this wide-ranging discussion in which Cardinal Lustiger confronts the outer crises of our times and the inner responses they produce. His inner responses are characteristically direct and consistent with his deep faith and commitment.

His originality is evident in the way he discusses another kind of suicide and another kind of temptation. He talks of suicide that afflicts a society and he warns of the "temptation to follow" — to follow everyone else, to follow the opinion polls, to follow along with the current consensus. Instead, he calls for Christians to follow Christ. Indeed, it's as much a demand as a call.

These reflections in March 1985 for a special issue of the French periodical France Catholique *have an enduring quality and an underlying message aimed at the year 2000, the end of the millenium. It is a message of faith filled with courage.*

---

*Translated by Jean-Denis Marzi, Ph.D.

Toward the Year 2000: Faith and Courage

Let's discuss the Western World in which we live and your warnings about our fate. You warn of suicidal tendencies. What do you mean?

I apply the term to our Western World, which was born out of Christianity, to describe the downfall we are witnessing today. It can have a wider meaning than the usual sense of individual suicide. It can identify a social problem.

Any attack on personal liberty, any denial of freedom, in short, any sin represents a form of suicide. Man has turned on himself and is destroying himself spiritually, dragging himself down into the abyss. Sin is a violation by the devil, as well as the source of spiritual death in man. The temptation in our world seems to lie there: we have forgotten the salvation of Christ.

Is this temptation found on the entire planet?

What one calls the Western World has now become universal. Science, technology, the models of political and economic democracy, the types of production and the means of communication involve a world based on manipulation.

But isn't this world — where man's knowledge and power have grown — a bearer of positive fruit?

Without doubt. The more man's power grows, the greater his power for doing good. However, man is tempted to abuse this power, putting himself in the role of creator. In fact, we have abused our powers, forgetting that our lives depend on God, man's Creator and Supreme Being.

Man's separation from God is a deep wound in the human condition, a wound of which man must be cured. We turn from God, and pride and its consequences rise up on our evil path: abuse of power, abuse of profit to the detriment of others, and a scorn for all human life. Lost, man reaps the fruits of death, even though he believes that he is working towards the expansion of life.

111

Famine in the world is a brutal example of this truth. I don't mean to say that natural causes for famine don't exist, but the consequences of sin are no less striking. The power men have accumulated in their hands today can remedy any plague the moment it manifests itself and the moment it is anticipated.

Do you see other signs of this waywardness?
A new understanding of human biology enables us to intervene in the human body as never before, permitting us to fight against a considerable number of illnesses. This means considerable good in favor of human life. But at the same time, we see a society immersed in death: from the death of human embryos through voluntary abortion and deadly experiments on the fetus to elimination of those who suffer from infirmities and murder of the elderly.

Rationality developed with the creation of sophisticated tools, extending directly by data-processing certain aspects of intelligence which double *ad infinitum*, like a mirror effect. It is an extraordinary expansion of the human spirit on its way to conquer the world. But as this rationality progresses, one can see that it runs the risk of becoming "one-dimensional," of becoming exclusive, and from there to stray towards a totalitarian identity.

At the same time, man has become capable of multiplying his means of sensory representation of the world. This could be used for a greater spiritual command of reality. Yet, strangely enough, what should be a rich understanding of reality acts like a drug which confuses man and even wounds him physically. Observe the new music. Doctors will tell you that certain young people, who listen regularly to rock music suffer ear damage. These are extreme cases, but significant nonetheless.

Finally, while man has been created for truth, beauty, and goodness, our information-saturated civilization does not know whom to trust. It lets advertising shape its sense of aesthetics and no longer believes in the fundamental difference between good and evil, or even worse, calls good what is evil.

The means of power have meaning only from values, and values only have weight if we know, ultimately, what man is. But do we know man's reason for existence, his goal, his completion, his end?

Does the Absolute impose itself upon man in the name of his humanity? Is there anything that can not be annulled, which never varies according to the hazards of history and culture, of opinion and social conditioning?

If nothing absolute imposes itself on man in the name of humanity, there is a vaccum which attests to the temptation of suicide. Then man is no longer man and reduces himself to the level of the things he manipulates, the animals he uses for his experimentation, the structure of the matter which he breaks up and recombines.

But man cannot find his identity by identifying himself with what is in his power. The light which could enlighten his conscience and show him that every human being is worthy of respect does not derive from that power. It infinitely exceeds it.

Take note of science fiction. It is revealing. It is somewhat like the daydreams of our civilization.

Does our civilization project itself in science fiction?

That's the right word. Our civilization projects its existential contradictions. Man wants peace, and the universe is full of conflicts and massacres. He desires truth, and the universe is full of deceit. He desires beauty, and the universe is full of horror. Finally, the inhuman universe continually transgresses what makes the humanity of man.

This imaginary world of science fiction warns us about the future. It cannot be compared with the pagan mythology of the ancient world. It is much more horrible! Ancient myths can be understood as a way to reflect on the human condition. It has been possible to take them up again, to correct them through the development of a rational and Christian thought. By contrast, modern tales reflect a conscience which is losing its direction. The humanity of man has no form therein.

Science fiction is not humanization of the animal universe that we see, but a beast-like transformation of the human condition. That phantasmagoria, which should attract more of our attention, reflects the inmost recesses of the minds. At present, reality is not far from it. For example, do we know what biologists could imagine and put into practice?

Wise biologists feel what Jean Rostand called "anxieties."

We have reached an alarming moment. In fact, the possibilities offered to us are such that we must ask again, with greater strength, the fundamental question: "Do we have a right to do what we have the capability of doing? Genetic manipulations have been done on animals. Do we want to do the same with man? Transgressing taboos is the mark of our time.

Taboos? In what sense?

Prohibitions which give the human species its structure. For example, those against incest and murder. They are not only based on social and biological imperatives. In the light of Divine Revelation and redeemed human reason, we acknowledge their fundamental justification in the Commandments, by which God opens to man a positive way to life and keeps him from wandering astray.

Not everything that man can do is good for him. We know it from Genesis: what man is capable of doing may bring him death and destruction. In our period of great confusion, we are losing the belief that there are things which morally can be done and others which cannot. In a word: good and evil. Our age is becoming insane, eager to legitimize anything at all.

What of atheism? Is it shaken in its self-conceit?

People are beginning to realize that atheism is a position of despair. We Christians can describe a civilization heading for disaster, and we are not surprised because we know that man must welcome redemption. To diagnose the disease is to open a door to a cure.

For fundamentally — to cite the Gospel — not every disease ends in death.

Precisely. What St. Paul has written at the beginning of the Letter to the Romans reveals in what way the man of today is ill. It is revealed so that man might be treated, cured, and saved. The difference between where we stand now and the 18th and 19th centuries is that humanity is beginning to realize it is ill. If the sick man becomes conscious of his state, the need to get out of it is awakened.

In this sense, our age is fascinating. At the very time when the risk of destroying ourselves has never been so great, men of today are conscious of the dangers and are looking for a way out. At the end of this millennium, from the bottom of his heart, man calls for help more than ever and is ready to open his eyes and his ears. The vigils spent in prayers by believers, their hopes, and their faith are not rejected by a wall of silence.

Then spiritual blindness and deafness are not as inevitable as in the past?

That condition is, in part, the result of sin. Christians must realize that the salvation offered by God makes us see what we did not want to see and hear what we did not want to hear. "Seeing they do not see, and hearing they do not hear."

The blinded sinner does not know that he is sinning. He does not know he is in darkness. For whoever is in darkness, the cure is to see; for the deaf, to hear and to understand. This is the first grace the Christian receives. It takes a long time to penetrate a hardened heart. It takes time for that heart to hear the Lord's question, "What do you want me to do for you?" and to answer like the blind men of Jericho: "Lord, let our eyes be opened."

In Christian life, much importance has been attached to social involvement. Today, one realizes that other questions demand attention before social involvement.

Involvement for the benefit of society is possible — sometimes obligatory — because of the spiritual force which makes it meaningful and without which it is empty. That is why reason, serving societies and their common good, needs itself to be saved. Human reason always runs the risk of becoming perverted.

It is extremely important for the progress of societies to cure human reason. The role of Christians is therein apparent. Through them, the intelligence called to the service of Christ starts searching for God. To the extent that believers are searchers for God, lovers of God, and mystics, man will be saved by his reason and will be able to use it in keeping with the dignity God grants him.

Isn't today's true struggle a defense of the humanity of man?

In the economic and social domains, we are no longer a partitioned society in which Christians constitute a subculture. Faith is identification with Christ. For the Christian, social engagement does not mean that one group serves another group. The specific struggle for Christians is no longer to demonstrate their own usefulness by fighting for others. Christians do not have to be auxiliaries or mercenaries of modern civilization.

Christians must realize where the real struggle lies in today's society. It is to defend the humanity of man. Christians will lead the struggle only if they conquer first in themselves the major temptations of that society so they can do the same in the social field. Then, with grace granted them to identify with Christ, they can be His witnesses.

How would you describe that true struggle?

Fundamentally, life in society brings forward the questions of liberty and temptation, dignity and degradation of man, good and evil, life and death. Such is the field where Christians must struggle to help their brothers to true victory. In the economic domain, what we know and preach is that material goods present a spiritual temptation and that there is a Christian way of poverty. It is not an economic theory, but a liberty to which man is called. The goods of the world should be means — not idols — to be used for the service of all, not a few. Christian poverty proceeds from the love of God and the conversion of the heart. As such, it is a liberating force.

Are we speaking of a sign of Christ?

Yes. Christians are a sign of Christ when faithful to the gifts granted them. They become like Him, one with Him, therefore, sharing His struggle. What Christ has done in the desert resisting temptations, on the cross in His Passion, through the gift of the Holy Spirit after His Resurrection, God continues in His sons, who are doing the work of the Son.

Perhaps economics and social problems seem far away from that essential struggle. But only if we remain on the surface of observable and measureable phenomena. Whatever means are used or theories applied, it is still true that the economic field implies a

116

relationship of man to the world. Man must constantly be freed from the golden calf, for, under different forms, "The golden calf is still standing."

What is said about money and economic goods must be said also about political relationships between men, about peace and war, as about relationships between people and their bodies. The struggle concerns all the domains where men are tempted not to be men anymore.

Christ, then, is the ideal for man.

It is in Christ, His Passion, and His Resurrection that the whole man is restored. That is why Christians have the strength to overcome this suicidal temptation with Christ, why by His Passion takes upon Himself what destroys us and by His Resurrection shows vividly God's Power in the victory over death.

It is with the strength of the Resurrected that we are called to the struggle in which human beings are at stake. Because of that strength, Christians have the audacity to confront immense and formidable powers with the obligation to tell abut good and evil and with the mission to remind everybody that there is a humanity of man created in the likeness of God and saved and raised by Him to a dignity that cannot be voided.

We give witness: "In this sense, the ideal of man is Christ Himself innocent, just, holy, compassionate, pardoning our sins, facing our death, risen from the dead, giving the Holy Spirit which is the beginning of eternal life."

"Here is the man," says Pilate: "He says the truth about man." It is truly the truth of the disciples of Jesus who follow Him in His passion. In all times His disciples are the best defenders of man, as soon as they welcome in union with Christ the force of God in the most devastating tests.

But people will only believe those words if Christians make themselves credible.

In a sense, it is not too important to be credible. One must believe. We have to be saints.

Saints never know that they are saints; they all tell you that they are horrible sinners. Never do those whom one calls saints esteem themselves better than other men by themselves. They say only that they owe everything to Him whom they have met, that God comes to pardon the sinners that they are, and that it is His grace which sanctifies gratuitously whoever accepts it. Every pardoned Christian must believe that he is sanctified by the grace of God. So I see, when I look at my own life, the immense patience that God has shown on my behalf to lead me to accept, so little and so badly, something of His goodness.

Therefore, what infinite patience should I not have toward my brothers in not pre-judging the way they may take! It is necessary to be a witness for the Word of God, for the love which it reveals, for the power of that love, for its work of fidelity. I have no need to seek to convince. It is God who convinces.

To be credible, it is necessary to believe, it is necessary to go as far as Christ on the cross, and to listen to this thief who says at His side, while another mocks Him: "For we [are condemned] indeed justly for we are receiving the due reward for our deeds; but this man has done nothing wrong. . . . Jesus, remember me when you will come in your Kingly power."

Let us hear, when Christ commends His life into the hands of His Father, the cry of the centurion: "Truly, this was the Son of God." It is love which rendered itself worthy of faith.

In the eyes of men and in the eyes of human conscience, where is the credibility and the efficacy of the martyr who gives up his life, if not in this supreme sign of the love to which we are called with him? He has no other convincing force than his fidelity based on the fidelity of God. It is God who makes of this buried seed the grain of the kingdom whose fecundity, in its most profound operation, escapes the eyes and makes one believe in Love.

Is this grain abundantly present in the world today through an incalculable number of witnesses and martyrs?
It is superabundant, it has always been so.

In judging history, are purely sociological terms enough to understand the past?

History is, for me, fascinating, because it is always the baffling history of salvation. There have always been immense currents of grace, immense ugliness, immense flowerings of beauty, immense deserts, and concealed domains which escape our understanding. Why, for example, were the Churches of Asia Minor and North Africa wiped out? Why are people most recently baptized showing astonishing fruits of grace? Such as people in various parts of Africa.

What is monumental for a Christian when he enters into prayer and considers the destiny of man is the innumerable crowd of his brothers. My heart is joyful, for example, when I think of Africans whom I have never seen, nor shall know, who are so far away in distance and culture, who are my brothers, nonetheless.

Still, aren't you concerned about the Church in the West?

I would be more concerned if my vocation were that of a manager in the public domain or as a political leader than I am as archbishop.

You say this in spite of the shortage of priests and of Christians in your churches?

Actually, we are struck by a kind of dramatic tension evident in the aggressiveness, the harshness of people, sometimes even murderous hatred. It is a strange time where one sees people turning in on themselves and losing confidence in life. We are preparing for ourselves frightening days to come. But, at the same time, a prodigious call of God must be recognized in this disturbed world. He opens doors which seem closed, doors of the heart, doors of conscience, doors of generosity.

God goes to seek His own where and how He wants. Often, there exists in the depth of beings, as in sleep, a mysterious reality which one did not suspect was there. It is none other than a seed of the Word and of the Kingdom of God. A seed sown long ago, sometimes thanks to a grandmother, to an educator or someone else, which one day bears fruit without one's expecting it.

What of martyrs in today's world?

At present, many Christians are in the situation of martyrs, not because of bloody persecution, but because of the solitude of faith.

If they want to be faithful to Christ in a strong and vigorous way, they are often obliged to declare themselves in contradiction with the common opinion of their contemporaries on numerous subjects, whether it is personal or social ethics. In the face of extraordinarily rapid fluctuations in the prevailing consensus, Christians must have a spiritual capacity of exceptional resistance.

Are you speaking of a particular kind of temptation, the temptation to follow?

Yes. The Christian identity resists the world. Look at what happened with infanticide and abortion. If one believes the polls, in the space of two or three years public opinion has see-sawed. Consider the problems of respect for the foreigner, of racism. Opinion is in the process of see-sawing. There are attempts to legitimize torture and massacres.

What is contrary to the law of God is in the order of mortal sin. Christians, who are obliged to uphold the law of God, will be perhaps misunderstood and vilified. Perhaps they will be martyrs in the sense I have just spoken of. But they are called to this courage, whatever the violence or the pressure of public opinion.

What in spite of everything is the final test of the believer?

It requires courage to call oneself in communion with the successor of Peter, with the successors of the apostles, with the assembly of the faithful, with the Church in its totality. It requires courage to love the Church, such as she gives herself, including the weaknesses of her members. Yes, that demands a courage, sometimes heroic, particularly when even some Christians say they are ashamed of the Church and, therefore, of themselves.

Such shame is spiritual suicide. Christians who are ashamed of the Church and belittle it are destroying themselves.

To dare to love the Church and to keep the pride and joy of being one of those she gathers is to share the love of Christ for her and the mission which was confided to her in this world.

PART III

REJOICE
IN THE CHURCH

Cardinal Lustiger is not a man or a church leader who sits on the sidelines. He sees himself and the Catholic Church as speaking moral and spiritual truth to power. Government aid for Catholic schools, abortion, racism, human rights — all these issues call for his active response. And respond he does, in thoughtful and unequivocal terms.

There is a particular type of rejoicing evident, not in controversy for controversy's sake, but in giving witness as Christian responsibility. He never swerves from the task of applying conscience to issues and of presenting the Christian perspective, particularly in the give-and-take of dialogue.

The sermons in the opening segment of Part III provide a backdrop for four dialogues, which in variety and scope present his vision and his forceful way of confronting issues that Catholics confront everywhere, particularly in democracies.

The Church
of the Living God*

In these six sermons, Cardinal Lustiger demonstrates how intently he himself hears the words of Scripture, both Old and New Testament. They are not abstractions, nor facile phrases to be quoted for the occasion. Neither are they words from another time in another place for other people and circumstances. The words live!

How and why they live for Christians as a community of the committed and of the believing — these are questions he discusses. He holds the questions up to the light of faith and thereby finds meaning and message, relevance and revelation.

To those who already believe, he shows the road toward greater conviction.

To those who already are dedicated, he points out the paths of greater commitment.

To those who already give witness, he stands forth as one eloquent voice among many voices, saying what all believers clamor to say, standing forth as do all true believers.

The Cardinal does not trifle. He proclaims — from celebrating the witness of martyrs to summoning all those who belong to the flock of believers. He proclaims the mission to stand witness with Christ as guide and shepherd.

---

*These sermons, delivered between September 7 and October 12, 1988, were translated by Jean-Denis Marzi, Ph.D.

I

Under the Patronage of the Martyrs

There are two important dates for the Church in Paris. On September 2, we remember the martyrs of Carmes, most of them Parisians. In 1792, they preferred to die rather than be unfaithful to the Pope and the Church. On October 14, we celebrate the Feast of St. Denis, founder of our Church here. The Church in Paris has kept alive the memory of its founding in the middle of the Third Century and the martyrdom of its first bishop, Denis, witness to the resurrected Christ.

What, then, is the connection between the martyrs and the life of the Church? Why attach such importance to martyrdom? In Greek, the word means, "giving witness to"; in Christian speech, especially by the sacrifice of one's life. In other words, death is a witnessing. But let us understand each other clearly.

Martyrdom, which is specifically Christian, is not a march toward death, despite appearances. In reality, it is rather a march toward life. It gives witness in its manner of dying that the life received from God is not lost with the physical destruction of the body. For, in this earthly life we are united in Christ's death and brought to life. Through sacrament and mystery, our body is transformed by Christ in the Glory of the Father.

Physically, the martyr is wounded, humiliated, and then massacred. By his faith, he reveals that he is free to live, until his last breath, in his devotion to God. This allows him to transcend physical existence and his human side and attain his vocation as a Child of God, as a Brother of Christ. For love of God he has the courage to face the worst fate in the eyes of man. He finds his reason for living, the ultimate sense for the trajectory of his life.

He accepts verbatim the counsel of Jesus to his disciples: "Do not fear those who kill the body but cannot kill the soul; rather, fear him who can destroy both soul and body in hell'' — namely, God our Father (Mt 10:28). He brings tidings. Amazing sign of a hidden reality. Christian martyrdom is the living Gospel.

The Christian martyr is a witness to love that forgives. He is opposite to the fanatic bred on hate who sacrifices his own life in the act of killing others. The Christian martyr reveals that Christ exists in him.

Christ loves and wants to save executioners and killers. He is the Savior of all men, and He ''came not to call the righteous, but sinners'' (Mt 9:13). The martyr reveals the force and beauty of love, which can even ''love your enemies,'' according to the commandment of Jesus (Mt 5:44).

Finally, Christian martyrdom reveals to us the *Church, the Body of Christ in the process of growing.* ''Christianity was born from the blood of the martyrs,'' said Tertullian. For, by sacrificing his life, the martyr reveals the Christ who lives in His brothers and acts in His body. He is a quasi-sacramental symbol of salvation through Christ's Passion.

Martyrdom gives birth to new disciples. Just as the Virgin Mary at the foot of the cross will henceforth pursue her maternity as an intercessor, aligning herself with her Son in glory. In Mary, we find the Church as Mother for all of those who become the brothers and sisters of Christ.

We can also understand why love of the Church characterizes Christian martyrdom. Those happy souls massacred in September 1792 attest that this love for the Church is based on faithfulness to the apostles whose cornerstone is the Pope, successor of Peter. Bishops and priests owe to the Body of Christ the faith that He has in them. For they were ordained for the good of others.

Today, as always, being faithful to the Pope guarantees our true unity in the Body of Christ. Through the martyrs as is expressed in the liturgy; ''The word of faith was planted in our hearts and born of their suffering and their blood.'' With them — for ''You cannot love more, Lord, than the unity and the freedom of your Church'' — may we bear witness without flaw to *the truth of the Word.*

II

'Coming Together' and 'The People of God'

The Church today is too often the scapegoat for all the resentments of our Western society. To speak of the Church in a more positive vein, let us use uplifting words.

The term "Church" is specifically Christian. It describes both a building and an institution. It comes from the Greek and means the gathering of those chosen by God: "A gathering in an assembly." Whoever says Church says a *coming together*. In the active sense, it is God who gathers and in the passive sense it means the group has come together at God's bidding.

Jesus Himself chose the word "Church": "On this rock I will build my church" (Mt 16:18). Greek translations from the Hebrew *"Gahal"* are used frequently in the Old Testament to describe a gathering of the people of God. That is why Vatican Council II (notably the constitution *Lumen Gentium*) has underscored the expression "People of God" among the names given to the Church. In the Old Testament, it describes the people of Israel. It is also used in this way in the New Testament.

How can we understand the "Church" as the "People of God?" We must break down these terms and relate their meanings to each other.

Although the term "people" is widespread in our language, its definition is not as simple as it seems. Is a "people" a nation? A linguistic group? A social stratum? In antiquity, the term "Roman People" was founded on Roman citizenship. For two centuries, French constitutional right used the term "the French People" to describe a group of citizens subject to national sovereignty. They are the base for the authority of the State.

Our civilization and our history have carved into our minds the political sense of "the people as a governing power" as well as "the will of the people," exercised by the right to vote and universal sufferage. In this way, the people delegate and are the governing authority. They have ultimate sovereignty.

Does the civic and social sense of France as a republic help us to better understand the biblical sense of the "People of God?" To say "People of God" is no longer to speak of a people turned in on themselves and their personal sovereignty. It is to say, *"God and the People," "The People and God."*

What is the rapport between the two? Is it the rapport of the sovereign to his subject? Does it describe a power struggle, in the old political sense of a ruler and his people?

Without knowing or wanting it, in our perception of the Church we call upon representations and ways of feeling that are likely to lead us into error, if they are not transformed by the fire of revelation. Think, for example, about the concept of king or royalty and its application to God ("God rules"); or to Christ ("You say I am a king"), Jesus' answer to Pilate (Jn 18:37); and even to the message in Scripture ("Blessed are the poor in Spirit, for theirs is the kingdom of heaven").

In order to answer these questions, we must further understand the definition of a gathered Church. The People of God are a people whom God gathers together. More precisely, the People of God were born through God's generosity. They were assembled, rather than gathered. Before being assembled by God they did not exist as a people. This people would have been scattered because of its sins. God took it upon Himself to assemble them. This gathering was presented by the prophets as an even greater manifestation of the love of God: new creation, new Exodus, resurrection of the dead. This is the divine work of our Creator and our Redeemer.

The Apostle Peter helps us to understand when he addresses the first community of the Church in the terms used for the people of the Old Covenant (cf. Ex 19:5-6). "You are a chosen race, a royal priesthood, a holy nation, God's own people. ... Once you were no people, but now you are God's people" (1 Pt 2:9-10).

III

The Birth of the People
of God

The Church is a "gathering" and the "People of God." How did this come into existence?

Answer: By the power of God.

1. This is illustrated clearly in the Bible by the story of Exodus, where all the ancient history of Israel is concentrated: "A wondering Aramean was my father [who, like the lost sheep, was on the verge of death]; and he went down into Egypt and sojourned there, few in number. . . . Then we cried to the LORD, the God of our fathers, and the LORD saw our affliction, our toil, and our oppression" (Dt 26:5-7). Those whom God was to pluck from enslavement by the Pharaoh are called a gathering, multitude, or rabble in the Bible (Ex 12:38; cf. Num 11:4). As in the parable of the wedding guests of the king's son, "the poor and maimed and blind and lame" were gathered from "the streets and lanes of the city" (Lk 14:21).

Here are the men and women God chose to be His people. He created them by saving them. The act of birth of the people of God is an act of salvation from death:"The LORD has taken you, and brought you forth out of the iron furnace, out of Egypt, to be a people of his own possession" (Dt 4:20). It is a people of escapees: escapees from servitude and idolatry.

However, while in flight in the desert, this people was faced with the hard apprenticeship of freedom given by God. Yes, for God must free man's heart from its desire to be enslaved, to be "a people holy to the LORD your God" (Dt. 14:2), a people invested with a sacerdotal mission, created by God to render Him homage. That is why the parting of the Red Sea appeared as a prophetic illustration of baptism: an act of rebirth and of deliverance.

2. "... the Lord set his love upon you and choose you, it is because our Lord loves you and is keeping the oath which he swore to your fathers" (Dt 7:7). To Abraham, God promised to multiply his "descendants as the stars of heaven" (Gn 22:17). Not only did He promise prosperous growth as a nation, but he blessed his people with a vow of fecundity, which was a promise of life and of sanctity.

This miraculous birth was founded on the covenant of God. As with the Virgin of Nazareth, at the moment of the announcement of the coming birth of Our Savior (Lk 1:37), the Angel of God answered Abraham and Sarah, who had passed the age of childbirth, with the words; "Is anything too hard for the LORD?" (Gn 18:14).

3. Finally, we can trace the birth of this people back to creation, when God said: "Let us make man in our image." (Gn 1:26). This plural sense reveals the life of the Divine Trinity in the communion of the Father, the Son, and the Holy Spirit. "He created both man and woman." The existence of a first "gathering" in praise of God, with the joy of communion and sanctity, is the creation of the first human couple.

The gathering of God's People is our Lord's desire to see all men saved. For human liberty shattered the original bond between man and God, his Creator. In this world confided to man to reign over creation, death appears at the hand of man: Cain kills Abel.

Henceforth, the blind forces of destruction and death seem to reign in this broken world. But God has not abandoned us to what looks like a fatal end. God, our only God, wishes to forgive sin, to cure our ills, to drive away death, and to give life. By assembling His people, God creates anew and gives us a new birth. This is the *work of our Lord*: a work which unceasingly gathers man scattered by sin in order to reunite him in communion with love.

Already, the story of the Tower of Babel has given us an idea of our present situation and that which is to come. Man's Promethean ambition to reach the heavens, to become his own master—in short, to make man the master of man — brings with itself the worst confusion: incomprehension and strife.

Men must acknowledge that their source of unity is greater than themselves. At Pentecost, the word of God—the burning tongue of flame of the Holy Spirit — becomes their common language amid the diversity of tongues and nations. It is at this moment, when the breath of the Holy Spirit embraces and consumes man in a rebirth of the Church, that the People of God are truly born.

IV

People of the New Covenant

How do Christians view their own Church?

We are often tempted to include the Church with other religious institutions of the world. After all, are not Buddhists monks the Asiatic version of the Benedictines? Voodoo priests the Haitian version of our country priests? In addition, in our secularized society — which substitutes for what is greater than man what tempts man, his desires — we are tempted to analyze the Church as any social system and thus reduce it to a game.

That is why it is important for Catholics to understand that there is much more in the Church. Its mystery cannot be based on an archaic religious phenomenon, nor can it be understood as a power structure. This would cut off the Church from its evangelical message and purge its reality. For the Church finds its source and its truth from something greater: from Christ, her Lord and Master.

What is the meaning, not only for ourselves but also for the history of humanity and the salvation of the world, of this Church of which we are — through grace — its members and its witnesses?

Remember what I said about the People of God. How does the Church appear in the eyes of faith?

1. As a New Creation

Eve, "mother of all living beings," came out of the hands of God. God made man the priest of creation. In the same way, the Church is the "New Creation" of God. The new Eve, the Virgin Mary, is prophecy, its figure and Mother.

2. As a New Birth

The birth of Isaac carried out the promise made to Abraham of countless descendants, "a great and mighty nation, and all the nations of the earth shall bless themselves by him" (Gn 18:18). This was the prophetic announcement of the birth of the Church. The Church has risen from a new birth. Jesus revealed to Nicodemus: "Unless one is born of water and the Spirit, he cannot enter the Kingdom of God" (Jn 3:5). The birth of Christians was already announced by the birth of the Son of the Virgin Mary. The new birth is carried out in the Sacrament of Baptism from which the Church is born.

3. As a New Assembly

The People of God, dispersed by sin and evil, were assembled by the Exodus to render homage to the Lord. At Pentecost, God assembles men and women of all nations, rendered capable by the Spirit of Christ of hearing the Word of God amid the diversity of human languages. They become the Church of Christ.

4. As the People of the New Covenant

The People of God found themselves, escaped servitude and death, and entered into the Promised Land, prophetic sign of the work of salvation: of the new and eternal covenant. The Church — brothers and sisters of Christ — is a redeemed people, based on the promise of universal redemption.

This was the teaching of the Fathers of Vatican Council II, following the words of Peter the Apostle (1 Pt 2:5ff). The Church has been singled out to "be a holy priesthood." Through Christ, the Church offers a unique sacrifice by which men, saved from sin and death, enter into a bountiful communion in the life of God.

This spiritual vision of the Church is not a vision of a dream superimposed on a human institution among others. It enables us to understand its basic origins. But the mystery of the Church only appears, as St. Paul tells us, when all of God's plan is revealed: "he [God] chose us in him [Christ], before the foundation of the world, that we should be holy and blameless before him. He destined us to be his sons through Jesus Christ. . . . In him we have redemption through his love. . ." (Eph 1:4-7).

St. Paul situates the beginning of the Church before the creation of the world: The world was created in terms of this Love of God.

In other words, the People of God were chosen since the birth of Israel to be the Church as long as history, the witness of universal salvation, lasts. By this unique grace, which is universally given, the Church is a private bond of trust between God and man.

V

The Presence of the Trinity's Love for Humanity

The greatness of the Church appears to us through its mystery: the salvation of man, fallen through sin but transformed by the presence of God.

Some say, "I believe in God, but not in the Church, or, "Scripture, Christ, as much as you want, but the Church, *no!*" Yet Christ, Our Savior, in His suffering and glorified humanity, cannot be separated from His disciples. The presence of Jesus to His brothers in His Church is the sacred revelation of God's Gift.

St. John tells us that he who pretends to love God but hates his brothers is *a liar* (cf. 1 Jn 4:20). We should say the same about love of Christ and love of His bride, the Church.

Here is our cornerstone, the test of truth and the strength of our faith or, on the contrary, of its weakness and its falsehood. A generation which only sees in the Church a social structure, an instrument of oppressive political power looking out for its own interests, has lost sight of the essentials and buries the treasure that God has given to us sinners.

In the tradition of the Church, the last Vatican Council stressed that there are three expressions which are inseparable when speaking of the Church.

● The People of God The Father.
● The Body of Christ His Son.
● The Temple of the Holy Spirit.

The Church is born of a mystery of love named the Holy Trinity. The Church has illustrated historically the mystery of the Incarnation, that is to say, the presence of the Word of the Father in this world, made real by the "Holy Spirit ... and the power of the Most High" (Lk 1:35). This fundamental birth has its roots in the chosen redemption of the People of Israel, to whom was given the "Word of God, the law, and the prophets."

People of God

The Father gathers "a people ... so that from east to west a perfect offering may be made," as the Third Eucharistic Prayer reminds us.

Body of Christ

This image is developed by the Apostle Paul. Jesus Himself announces it in his discourse on the Pain of Life (Jn 6:22ff). St. Luke (2:7), emphasizes that the Body of Christ was placed at its birth in a "manger." To become like an infant, born from *on high*, but also to have known the pains of labor. Such is the vocation of the Church. It is both the People of God, born from the baptismal water and the Spirit of Pentecost, and the mother who gives birth in the suffering of the Passion.

To recognize in the Church the Body of Christ is to believe that it cannot be dissociated from the Christ-Head, to whom we belong. This union is illustrated by our faith in the Eucharist.

Temple of the Holy Spirit

The Church is the new Temple prophesied by Ezekiel (40-48). Divine work, a temple built of sacred and marvelous stones, "living stones" (1 Pt 2:5), men and women, baptized in Christ, a new assembly of people under the one dwelling place of God: the Church, the Sacred Temple. Not only does God make it His home, but the stones themselves are inhabited by the Holy Spirit.

Thus, to speak truthfully about the Church one must use three images jointly: People of God, Body of Christ, Temple of the Holy Spirit. For the Church receives its existence and its life from the Father, the Son, and the Holy Spirit.

That is why we must understand that the Church is the sacrament of love, the place of God-given *love*. Born of the will of the Father who gathers His People, born of the redemptive act of Christ who makes us part of His Body, born of the power of the Holy Spirit who gathers us into a sacred temple where God makes His home, the Church is the revelation of the eternal mysterious love of the Father, the Son, and the Holy Spirit. Love is a gift, an exchange, a communion. It is a love whose signs we feel in this life through our human relationships of filial, paternal, and maternal love as well as fraternal love.

This supreme love of God is always given freely to men through the Church. It is "in Christ, as in the sacrament, that is to say, the means and the sign of the intimate union between man and God and the union of the entire human race" (*Lumen Gentium* 1).

Whoever talks of union with God and the unity of men talks of the secret of *love*. The secret of the Church.

But, you reply, among Christians we speak evil of each other. How can it be that we love each other so little if the Church is a mystery of *love*?

Because we only love each other when constantly shown love. God, who is rich in mercy, constantly takes our hand gathering us to Him: "Come, you have strayed: Open your heart to the forgiveness I give you. Forgive. Love, for you are loved."

VI

The People of God,
the People of His Flock

The mystery of the Church is found in the Holy Trinity. Through the Holy Spirit and in Christ, God manifests the design of His love.

People of God, Body of Christ, Temple of the Holy Spirit — inseparable titles. We have yet to discover the different facets of each title: How, in the term People of God, the Father, the Son and the Holy Spirit are present. How God the Father creates and gives life to the Body of Christ. How, in the Temple of the Holy Spirit, the Father shows the greatness of the Creator, Father of Jesus Christ, in whom the richness of the love of the Holy Spirit is infused.

In the first Psalm of the "Office of Lauds," we sing: "Come, let us cry for joy for our LORD. . . . For he is our God, and we are the people of his pasture, and the sheep of his hand" (Ps 95:1,7).

The Psalm about grace recaptures in a poetic way the theology of the People of God, fashioned by its experience through Exodus and its priestly vocation. It identifies the People of God as the "Flock of God."

Remember the Scriptures, especially the words of Jesus. Remember His parable of the lost sheep: "And he has found it, He lays it on his shoulders, rejoicing" (Lk 15:5). And in St. John (10), you know how Jesus presents Himself: "I am the Good Shepherd . . . Truly, I say to you, I am the door of the sheep." He does the work of God: He gathers His dispersed flock and becomes the Shepherd of His People. In effect, the People of God, become His flock because God reveals Himself as Shepherd and Redeemer in His Son.

This work of Christ in commanding God's flock is at the same time the work of the Holy Spirit, who will abide in God's People. The Holy Spirit will give them unity and help them recognize the voice of the one and true shepherd: "My sheep hear my voice, and I know them, and they follow me." It is thanks to the Holy Spirit that we can know Jesus and realize that He knows us. It is the Holy

Spirit who can help us to know our identity.

Christ promised His disciples: "When the Spirit of truth comes, he will guide you in all the truth. . . . You will know that I am in my Father, and you in me, and I in you. (Jn 14 and 16—*passim*). Vatican II also said: "The Holy Spirit gives all of Christ's disciples the desire and the motivation to join all of God's people in a peaceful union, in one flock and under one shepherd (*LG* 15). "The Spirit maintains all of God's flock in the unity of faith" (*LG* 25).

Vatican Council II also stated: "Under many images is the true and intimate nature of the Church revealed" (*LG* 6). These symbolic representations of spiritual realities also provide access to the fundamental aspects of both Revelation and our existence.

The Church is "the flock to which Christ is the sole entry. It is also the flock to which God announced beforehand that He would be its Shepherd (cf. Is 40:11; Ex 34:11). Although its sheep are led by human shepherds, they are nonetheless guided and nourished by Christ Himself, both the Good Pastor and the prince of shepherds (cf. Jn 10:11; 1 Pt 5:4), who gave His life for His sheep" (*LG* 6).

Describing the Church in this way helps us to assess human history and to situate the Church in its relation to all humanity created by God, to know it, love it, and serve it (cf. Dt 11:12). This biblical image of the flock applied to the Church reveals — within the universality of God's plan — the identity and destiny of God's people. Creator and Redeemer of all men, God has chosen one people, and He gathers His flock in view of everyone's salvation and gives to all His love. The Messiah, Eternal Son made man, is the Shepherd.

Calling the Church "God's flock" shows us its place in the world and thereby our own relation to the rest of humanity, as members of this Church, immersed in its destiny as a priestly people. "By our mission all baptized members are called to gather under one flock so as to render together homage to God, their Lord, before all nations" (Missionary Activity to the Church, *Ad Gentes* 6).

The Rampart of Faith*

This interview by Jean Bourdarias, a prominent French journalist and author on religious affairs, begins with a poignant reference. When asked about France's celebrated Declaration of the Rights of Man, the cardinal turns immediately to the reaction of a famous French author when his wife described the carloads of Jewish children sent to their deaths by the Nazis during their occupation of Paris.

The Cardinal could have been one of those children.

His mother died in a concentration camp.

No facile celebration of the Rights of Man for the cardinal, who personally experienced the denial of those rights and who warns that the debate over human rights "has just begun."

As ever, the cardinal is consistent. He points in the direction of God and His revelations as the foundation on which to build human rights.

He is not only inspirational in this lively exchange. He demonstrates his special ability to address contemporary issues from a religious position without diluting his religious principles or mixing politics and religion. For Cardinal Lustiger, it is not the Church which must get in step with the current debate on human rights, but the debate which must get in touch with its Christian roots.

---

*Published in the Autumn 1988 issue of *Politique International*. Translated by Jean-Denis Marzi, Ph.D.

The Rampart of Faith

In celebrating the bicentennial of the French Revolution, France is also celebrating the Declaration of the Rights of Man and the Citizen. What about the attachment that our generation has for the rights of man?

This reminds me of a text by François Mauriac that appeared in 1958 in the preface of the first book by Elie Wiesel: *The Night*. During the Nazi occupation of Paris, Mrs. Mauriac, coming back from the Austerlitz Station, tells her husband that she just discovered a carload of Jewish children leaving for the East. Here is the passage:

"I had not seen them with my own eyes, but my wife described them to me, still full of the horror that she had felt. We were ignorant at the time of Nazi methods of extermination. And who would have thought of them? But these lambs torn from their mothers, this went beyond anything that we would have thought possible. That day, I think I touched upon, for the first time, the mystery of iniquity whose revelation marked the end of an era and the beginning of another. The dream that Western man had in the eighteenth century, and whose climax he thought he saw in 1789; which, up until August 2, 1914, had strengthened itself through Reason and Science; this dream crumbled for me in front of these wagons crammed with little boys. And I was miles away from thinking that they were headed to the gas chambers and crematoriums."

These words confirm in the eyes of justice what the Western World feels today, faced with the rights of man. The great hope which during the Age of Reason exalted man's greatness and dignity has become, two hundred years later in the name of reason, its exact opposite. The universal declaration of 1948 tried, following the Second World War, to reassemble the pieces of this broken promise. Yet the debate about the foundation and content of the rights of man in the contemporary world has just begun.

What does this debate consist of?

One of the worst dangers for humanity would be to scuttle the pursuit of a universal foundation for the rights of man. For the rights of man must have an authority which precedes and commands other laws and cannot be swayed by public opinion or propaganda. If not, it would suffice, for example, to obtain a majority vote to decide that torture is a legitimate means of interrogation by the police or an acceptable sanction by justice. Would this law respect the rights of man? And if abortion or euthanasia are legal practices in certain countries, must we conclude that this is moral and one does not have the right to be born or to die?

Experience shows us that the law is not sufficient to establish a state of righteousness conforming to morality and respecting the rights of man.

Does the Church have a specific message concerning the rights of Man?

The Church bases the authority of its faith on a philosophical affirmation often challenged: Human nature is correctly defined when we emphasize the human person. In other words, all men possess equal dignity because each is a human being. There are, therefore, universal and inalienable rights demanded by the nature of Man, which apply beyond any particular political system. This affirmation is based on the divine revelation found in the Bible: God created man in His image. All men are brothers through their creator. Consequently, they all have the same fundamental rights.

For the Church, a central core of human rights exists, rooted in the condition of man, made in the image of God. Even more, faith in Christ the Redeemer of Men underscores the unity of the human race and makes even more unconditional the respect which is due each individual in it.

The disciples of Christ are actually the only ones to preach the universality of human rights, which is not only the result of conventional recognition of states. The Church is the only worldly institution which, beyond political, cultural, and ideological frontiers, preaches that each man must see his equal in other men. Jesus gives us the definition in the parable of the Good Samaritan: My equal is not my nearest neighbor so much as the wounded stranger I approach in order to give him the dignity which others, passing by, refuse him. This Christian vision of the other is exactly opposite to the notion of the tribal or the ethnic.

Love and respect for all men engenders in Christians a singular behavior: martyrdom, not provocative suicide, nor suicidal aggression, nor fanatical exaltation. Thus, the martyr — the word means witness — is neither a hero nor a guerrilla. He bears witness to the love of God for all men. He accepts death with Christ so that pardon and reconciliation will triumph.

Considering the cultural and ideological diversity of the regions of the world where the Church exerts an influence, is it not sometimes necessary to set aside the principle of universality that you just described and adapt a more concrete localized version of the rights of man?

One does not do the universal aspect of inalienable human rights any injustice by recognizing the diversity of the conditions in which they are applied. For example, to determine the right to work or the right to health makes no sense unless we take into account the medical equipment or the level of economic development of each nation. Yet the inequalities require, in conscience, that we work toward reducing them for the good of all.

The Church holds an original position, often not understood, by affirming that there is one fundamental right which commands all others: the right to religious freedom, or, if you prefer, the right to freedom of conscience.

Religious freedom is, in effect, the root of all human rights. For man has received the power and the duty to address himself to someone greater than man and to worship Him, namely God. God judges the master and the slave, the governor and the governed, those who command and those who are commanded, those who make the laws and those who obey them. The Christian bears witness that there is a judge in heaven: It is the guarantee of our freedom on earth. The Church, if it is faithful, is the main obstacle to all tyranny. That is why it suffers constant persecution. Men belong to God and not to society, nor to the state, nor to the ruler. And, this irritates society, the state, and the ruler.

Independent of ideology?

Yes. For the rule of ideology is the strongest that exists. A tyranny can be brought down while its ideology can survive, even without a tyrant. It is to Orwell's credit to have shown, in *1984*, that Big Brother need not exist and yet he still rules. For ideology is so depersonalized that it fits like a leaden mold over all who fall its victim.

Let's address current situations. In Poland, the Church was led for very diverse, historical reasons to manifest itself on the political scene by joining the Solidarity movement. Meanwhile in Nicaragua, it is opposed to priests in the government. How can you explain this apparent contradiction?

In fact, these positions are less contradictory than they seem.

Poland has been repeatedly enslaved and torn apart by its neighbors. Its political existence has on many occasions been hampered and overturned. Over the centuries, it was the Church that was the soul of the Polish nation. Since the end of the Second World War, a deep division was created between the communist state and the historical and cultural reality of the country. The Church has tried to reduce this division, but it has not always been easy.

Regarding the Solidarity Movement, the Polish Church has constantly pointed out—as well as the Pope when he traveled to Poland —that the Church must help the Poles acquire a legitimate political expression, but that it must not be a spokesman for union demands. Church authorities have reminded priests that they must in no way directly assume political functions, be they elective or governmental. The same message has been sent to Nicaragua. From this point of view, there is no contradiction in the Church position.

From what you say, there is consistency rather than contradiction.

Exactly. The Church refuses to become a political instrument in whatever country it might be. In the same way, the Church refuses to gain power in order to set up a theocracy. It is difficult to maintain a balance, I assure you.

You say that the role of the Church is not to intervene in

political affairs. But when Pope John Paul II visited Port-au-Prince in Haiti, did he not declare: "Things must change here." Doesn't this strike you interference in the internal affairs of the state? In this specific case, did he not risk destabilizing a regime without even proposing a political substitute?

The Pope said: "Something must change here." This "something" is the misery of the people, deprived of freedom and even basic rights. Beyond a change of regime, a deep reform in society is needed. Because of the corruption of their leaders, the richest and most educated Haitians have fled their country to live in the United States or France. The only elite who remain in Haiti and support the poor people are the clergy. In accordance with international organizations, the Church is coordinating numerous humanitarian and literary campaigns.

Is this overstepping bounds? Is it going over the head of the Minister of National Education? In reality, the priests are only doing what all priests in the world have always done: They are helping people to live and they are giving their own lives and doing so for the love of Christ. When Mother Teresa helps the dying, does she infringe on the duties of the Indian Minister of Health?

Between an authoritarian regime on the Right, which may soon disappear, and a totalitarian regime from the Left, which is hard to get rid of, where does the Church's position lie?

If we suppose that the Church would make such a choice, it does not have the means to legitimately intervene on a political level. In addition, it is rarely faced with this choice. Finally, in situations where priests are confronted with force and a concrete reaction is called for, they are required to face them, not in terms of political violence, but in spiritual terms. The Church, when faced with political calculation, upholds the absolute belief in Good versus Evil and even asks some of its sons to have the courage to accept martyrdom. It is the martyrs who have broken the strongest chains and have overcome the biggest obstacles. Might I remind you of my thought on this: "Neither hero nor guerrilla, but martyr."

Getting back to the Declaration of the Rights of Man, we know

that it was drawn up in an anti-Christian spirit. How can the Church, without any second thoughts, associate itself with the bicentennial celebration of the French Revolution?

It was from a Christian root that two centuries ago the hope of those generous men was nourished as they cried out for liberty and equality. Today, this Christian origin seems to have disappeared, and the ideals which inspired the authors of the declaration seem to have lost their meaning to most of our contemporaries.

Therefore, the problem is not to reconcile the Church with the ideals of the Revolution, but to maintain its true effectiveness in line with the original intention of the eighteenth century which has been disrupted by crisis and war. It is to instill renewed Christian Spirit in keeping with the original inspiration.

The Church Obeys God, Not Men*

Journalist Christine Clerc of the politically conservative Paris newspaper Le Figaro begins this interview with a revealing description of Cardinal Lustiger. What follows in the interview is a forceful statement of how the Church gives witness in the contemporary political area. The cardinal practiced what he preached in two controversial episodes: the first was a court fight over the schools in which the cardinal successfully defended the integrity of Catholic schools against government interference; the second was over the racist political campaigning of Jean-Marie Le Pen. The questions and answers begin after this preface by journalist Clerc.

A peaceful Sunday afternoon at the archbishop's headquarters in Paris. In the courtyard of the great provincial-style house, Vietnamese children dressed like English pupils are playing — the superintendent's children. A staffer leads us up an old flight of stairs to the second floor to the cardinal's office, filled with his books. Dressed in black corduroy suit with thick crepe-soled shoes, the cardinal gives the impression of a forceful, stocky peasant, a little rough on the edges.

A year ago, when I came to see him in the midst of the school battle, I found a man "crucified." "The proceedings against us," he had said to me, "are the same as those brought against Christ. — 'You are not the friend of Caesar — Who made you King?' It is normal that one speaks ill of us, that one crucifies us, since we, the bishops, are the witnesses of Christ."

Today, during the Le Pen controversy, I find an angry man. Angry

---

*Published March 23, 1985, in *Le Figaro*. Translated by Jean-Denis Marzi, Ph.D.

because he "has had enough" of this racism, of this hatred, of this violence that is developing in France. Enough of the egoism of the industrial world and of the famine in Africa. Angry, also, because of the Christians and others who call you the Bishops to "mind their own business," while at the same time pressing them more and more, to join in political debate. Journalists want them to comment on all the burning issues.

"One takes me for a tube of mayonnaise," he sighs, making me sit at his formica table and consulting his watch, anxious not to be late for his appearance on Radio Notre-Dame for his 6:30 p.m. Mass in Notre Dame.

In order to relax him a bit, I suggest a little sun, to go down and take a picture with the children.

"Ah! No," he grumbles. "I don't want to do pictures. I am not *The Night of the Caesars*—."

"Come now, *Monseigneur,* you know very well that you are a star!"

I mention a political star who also makes a fuss about being photographed. That makes him smile, and — although with rather poor grace—he consents to go down, "But just for a minute." And there he is, talking with the children in the courtyard, squatting to be on their level, suddenly perfectly at ease, astonishingly relaxed. Back in his office, I question him first about his political role.

Does the fact of possessing political power bother you? How do you answer to those who advise bishops "to mind their own business"?

The underlying idea behind such remarks is this: There is no morality, there are only customs. It is the pagan conception of social life. For them, religion is made to make customs sacred. Religion is very important in order to mobilize energy: the emperor must have the sacred at his service.

But the proper sense of Revelation is that there are absolutes which determine the life of man. There is a good, and an evil, which concern societies as much as individuals. The predominance of the state is an abomination. The political domain is no more separated from morality than any other domain of human activity. All will be judged by God. To say this is not to threaten but to save man. For God alone is God and man is made for God.

That a call to ethics may have an influence proves that man is not an animal. I have the right and the duty to speak according to my responsibility and under the aspect of moral and religious conscience. This involves a problem, of course. I must be circumspect. It is not easy to express oneself with clarity so as to be understood. But is there a morality? Yes or no? I say that one cannot defend the good with instruments of evil.

Even if the adversary starves, tortures, crushes? One cannot torture to save the lives of children?

No! Otherwise, the adversary succeeds in making you his accomplice. Otherwise, as the price of life we lose our reasons for living. One cannot accept anything at all. One cannot agree to debase oneself. They are formidable, the people who would be holy.

You are thinking of Poland?

For example, yes. That which the police do not succeed in doing in Poland—the debasement of a people—may alcohol not achieve! Actually, I was thinking of martyrs in general. The blood of the martyrs is the seed of Christians.

But haven't so many sacrifices been in vain? Have they changed the frightful disorders of the world?

Where are the Caesars? Would you tell me what is left of the Caesars? The least Vietnamese child, the obscure woman dying in a hospital can share the identity of the martyred Christ. Emperors only leave ruins. Hitler is dead! The Christians are living. Christianity is the only force capable of resisting and of saying that the Colossus has feet of clay.

Perhaps. But Christians did not know how to prevent either Nazism or totalitarianism or the growth of fanatical Islam. I wonder sometimes if Christian democracies are not condemned by their weakness to be crushed, if the Christian faith is really weakness. A sentence in your book _Dare to Live_ startled me. "In

the face of terrorism," you write, "It is necessary to trust in intelligence, in strength, and in pardon." I do not trust, I am afraid.

Do you know that this argument about the weakness of Christianity has been used since the appearance of Christianity? It has not stopped, all the way to Nietzsche. Yet it is those who accuse Christianity of weakness who have produced Nazism and totalitarianism. It is the Western rationalist apostasy which is the source of horrors.

You insist that "the illnesses of Europe have something specifically Christian in their roots." You speak of the perversion of Christian values, but never of evil. The devil, evil — they exist nontheless?

Yes, there is a mystery of the devil. We believe that man can resist the devil. But I wanted to speak, above all, of the sin of those who have received the light. A saint falls from a greater height. He who has come close to God can move furthest from Him.

Indeed, it seems that for you the decline of Europe and the cause of all our evils are tied to this distancing from God, to this aberration of Christian faith.

Yes. Faith exalted human reasoning in liberating it. Reason, modern rationalism, was nonetheless born in this narrow region where Revelation was nourished. (*With his two hands he forms a triangle whose point could be Israel, and the sides those of the Catholic Roman empire.*)

The arrival of the knowledge of God produces at first positive fruits in liberating man, but afterwards modern rationalism produces materialism, the refusal of God, Marxism.

You write: "In order to cure evil, one has to return to a common source. Mankind must retrace its way backwards, and understand at what place it went wrong."

Yes. One must return to the place where it went wrong.

In the third century? In the twelfth century? In the sixteenth century? This place, do you situate it historically?

No. The temptations have been fundamentally the same all along the way. They are the very temptations of Christ. But the social consequences vary. Who have been the prophets of modern times? Small children like Bernardette Soubirous. At the dawn of a terrible century, these small children say: "Attention, here are the ones who will be the victims."

A detail moved me very much at Lourdes: Bernadette ate some grass. I believed I saw there a prophetic sign in the manner of the Old Testament, a kind of mime, a prefiguration of what humanity will become in the course of this century. Men reduced to the level of beasts.

It's a very bleak world that you're predicting for us in the long run. The disappearance of moral conscience, the perversion of science. Don't you also see some signs of hope?

What I see is that we are living. We would be in a desperate situation if God had completely left the game. As long as there remains one believer, there will be a seed.

And what of the youth and the development of all the new Christian communities. Don't they give you hope. Why don't you speak to me about them?

Modesty prevents me. I believe it, but I do not know it.

The Church and Public Life*

The cardinal's vision invariably carries him beyond the here and now, the parochial and the specific, the passing reference and the immediate issue. This exchange with Philippe Tessor, director of the Paris publication Quotidien, *is a stirring example.*

The starting point is elections in France. The outcome is a broad view of how Catholics and their Church give witness in the public life of a democracy in Europe or North America. Talk not to the cardinal of quick fixes and party slogans, and if you try, he will respond by citing the underlying Christian values of Western society, the moral issues that individuals cannot evade, and the vital place of religion.

In particular, Cardinal Lustiger rejects and resists any attempt to put the Church on the sidelines. Or to use it for purposes other than its God-given mission. The Church, he emphasizes, is not around to be used when it suits the occasion. Its unremitting witness is integral *to society. And he explains how and why.*

During any election, the Catholic vote is always discussed. Before any such discussion, a question needs asking: whether in view of the drop in religious practice Catholics carry any weight in the first place. What do you think?

Catholics have put the best of themselves into participating in the game of democracy in France, despite the great torments of internal and external conflicts. They have worked to avoid confusing religious adherence with a partisan politican attitude. They have consistently differentiated what pertains to the demands of moral conscience and must be translated into the political plane from what

*Published April 15, 1988, in *France Catholique*. Translated by Jean-Denis Marzi, Ph.D.

belongs to the spirit of factionalism. Just when generations of Catholics have arrived at this clarification, some people challenge their place in political life. I find that completely inconsistent.

Is there a Catholic vote? It is difficult to determine in a pluralist France, where conflicts have calmed down on a number of major points. The political weight of Catholics manifests itself in their vigilance concerning the moral stakes in political life. It counts in another and sometimes stronger way than formerly, when it was measured by the number of "Catholic votes." Now, it is reflected in the national conscience, where the position of the Church intervenes as a factor, sometimes a decisive one.

It is more fragile and delicate to appeal to the freedom and conscience of all citizens than to appeal to the discipline of the party, even on a so-called Catholic basis. It is a way of acting, perhaps, more profound, more efficient, and more respectful of people. Machine-like men prefer partisans or poster-hangers who fight before thinking. The Church does not furnish either. It asks each one, whatever his political affiliation and religious situation, to reflect, not only with his reason, but with his moral conscience.

Sometimes the position of the Church receives a favorable welcome, either because it coincides with a general sentiment or because it evokes something that was dormant in the conscience of a people. Our difficulty is not to act upon political power, but to avoid being enslaved by it. The Church does not follow anyone's bidding. For their part, politicians must take into account moral factors.

What are the sensitive points of our society from the viewpoint of this moral conscience?

It is difficult to distinguish between the secondary and the fundamental in western political life amid the periodic renewal of governments. Rarely are the long-term ends of a society taken into account, unless it is thanks to the conscience of someone. Long-run ends rest more on the nation itself. The Church, by its structure and because of its permanence and stability, is more sensitive to the long run.

For example: Family structures and the solidity of the family are constituent elements of all social life. Their evolution can only be measured over several generations. When a society de-institution-alizes the union of man and woman and family relationships, it is a certain sign of social breakdown, and its corresponds with a moral breakdown. The decline in marriage is a sign of alarm for the survival of society; it is a moral problem, not just a problem of political or governmental technique.

The temptation of politicians is to promise that in the span of two years they are going to settle basic questions which demand a half-century and the moral reform of a nation. Politicians are not prophets, priests, philosophers, moralists; they are only political men. They are the managers of social coherence and of the daily functions of life. They are not substitutes for the moral conscience of citizens. They must, on the contrary, listen to it, obey it, and assist it to the extent that they can. The makers of law are not to determine what is good and what is evil. They must arbitrate the conflicting interests which come up against the need to do good and the refusal to do evil.

You asked about the sensitive points in our society. At the very root, the problem of education is major. I am not promoting a system that adapts the young to the work market. Education in the noble sense is one of the fundamental characteristics of the human species. A human being does not attain his real historical stature if he does not gather from his parents and the generations that preceeded him the memory of values which constitute humanity. The human species is the only one in which being is in part undetermined because it is not pre-programmed. Therefore, to educate is to trans-mit something that does not come from social determinism but which relates to liberty and its flowering. A human being is spiritual-ly poverty-stricken if he knows nothing of his history.

Moral conscience itself is learned. The mastery of man over the universe is learned. Presently, we are witnessing a breakdown of the system of transmission, and the problem of education is the major problem of all Western societies. This involves the manner by which generations will be able to recognize each other, to agree with past generations, to transmit the patrimony of humanity. That plays upon moral values: to know what is good and what is evil. This plays upon memory. Where do we come from? Why?

That affects the spiritual treasure, which, for the people who have received Revelation, is knowledge of the word of God. That encompasses the fundamental values of mutual relationships, respect for one another, the will to live, the fundamental values of family life. We know, very well, that these values are transmitted not by passive inheritance, but by active identification.

When a society is depraved, it cannot transmit honesty to its children. When a society lives in falsehood, it cannot transmit the taste for truth, unless by accident. When a society lives in a dream (as in the media universe), it cannot transmit the sense of the real. If it does so, it will be at the price of a rupture. Sons will revolt against their fathers. That's what is happening!

Other problems stem from this. Developed societies, through scorn for philosophical reflections, end up by reducing the human body to a pure object. The result is moral panic in the face of the power which men have over the body of man. Genetic manipulations and respect for life in its terminal phase are among a multitude of questions of which we see only the beginning. While it would be absurd to play with fear in order to reject technological progress, it is time to appeal to the moral conscience of all. Humanity cannot deliver its destiny into the hands of those who manipulate technique.

Another problem concerns the mutual respect of men for one another. In private, most politicians point out that within fifty or a hundred years we are going to witness great migrations. One can react as did the decadent Roman Empire, with the feeling that others are barbarians and that one must either defend oneself or yield. And since a weakened people is not capable of defending itself, it ends by yielding. One can also react as did the Christians of those centuries by the force of faith, of love, of hope.

History does not repeat itself, but there are analagous situations. How to master this situation which is ours? I have not spoken thus far of the family because it seems to me tied to the preceeding points. It is too easy to condemn without efficacy. Everyone easily sees that it is scandalous to publicize lies about prostitution, about erotic use of the body of man and woman, about apologies for all the vices. But I take that as an effect, much more than a cause. Such a disorder is possible when morals have already crumbled. A breach has been opened, a breach in conscience. When a population is a moral accomplice, things that are morally bad become possible, because they are legitimized. Evil has always existed among men, but judgment about evil has varied according to the times.

When a nation holds that there are no more rules to observe in transactions and when morals are corrupted, methods of enforcement are not enough. In the struggle against drugs, repressive measures count, but they are not enough when love of money and disrespect for others are the rule. If one closes one door, the traffic will pass through another. The moral conscience of a people is an immunizing system that gives each one the power to react freely and to choose good rather than evil.

You have spoken of the audio-visual media and how they fabricate dreams. Haven't they taken on new dimensions in recent years? How do you judge this phenomenon?

I am very hesitant. The means of communication are prodigious and, yet, perverse effects are visible. In the psychic sense they are similar to tranquilizers. The effect upon individuals is perhaps more harmful because they deaden than because they tempt. The cinema offers the spectator what he desires. The image at arm's length prevents him from exercising inner discernment.

Man is free to choose his thoughts, except when he is in a state of obsession, of struggle, or of crisis. We are educated — it is our nobility — to direct our thoughts. The impact of television is that we no longer direct them. We let our sight and hearing be guided by others. The only power that we have is to choose the programs or to shut off the set. One must not forget the prodigious hold of the senses over the mind, especially when such a habit is socially legitimized. However, television can permit, conversely, positive communication. For that reason, it is necessary that television viewers be educated.

Sociologists explain to us today that individualism is the destiny of the West. We will never return to the organic societies of the past. If the individual is our destiny, one deduces the

relativity of all norms measured according to individual desire. What do you think?

If one opposes the social and the individual as two realities that must fight against each other and exclude each other, one forgets that there is no strong individualization except in relation with another and in the awareness of this relation. In this respect, Christianity has historical experiences which are interesting to consider. The monastic and the anchorite tradition can help us to understand contemporary movements. Monks, and even more the solitary, have given us the example of sovereign affirmation of the personality in solitude, while, in their case, it was a question of the highest interiorization of "social" norms. The hermit lives for the Church and by the Church, in obedience to the Church, personally represented by a superior. The solitary cannot subsist without becoming mad, unless he integrates within himself the totality of the history of the world and of his salvation.

The logic of Western society goes toward individualization, not to the detriment of social coherence, but to found it on reality. The liberating experience of the sovereignty of liberty establishes the communion of persons, breaking the tribalism of social behaviors. However, the conditioning of the media reestablishes this tribalism. The fluctuations of fashion are altogether impressive. The annual decrees of the venders of fashion constitute an astonishing conditioning of social life. It is the reappearance of the gregarious instinct under its most archaic form. It is all the more strong in that individuals are less armed to resist.

A final question. What place does the Church claim in public debate and public life?

Everyone agrees. The Church does not claim any privilege for herself. What she says to the whole nation constitutes the conscience of the nation. We do not pretend to exclusivity. We give witness as guarantors of that which founded our civilization. If the norms of social life dictated by the political and administrative power do not permit the Church and Catholics to express themselves, it is the nation that is in danger. We do not claim a liberty only for ourselves. We think that this liberty is necessary for the life of the nation, for its future. We do not defend our interest as would a pressure group, but we fulfill a duty regarding the whole of society.

We are not gurus that one brings out of the closet when they seem useful. The Church exists only in relation to the real life of people. We ask that one recognize religious values as an integral part of civil society.

The Church
and Democratic Rights*

In the midst of France's bicentennial celebration of its Revolution, Cardinal Lustiger issued a stunning reminder to his countrymen and the world: religious liberty is the foundation for all other liberties. He did so at a particularly sensitive time: when the French were celebrating the 200th anniversary of an upheaval that centered on secularism and martyred priests and bishops.

The cardinal chose an attention-getting platform to place the French Revolution of 1789 in perspective. He engaged in a bold dialogue with historian François Furet, who had captured the attention of France with his best-seller The Revolution. *The prestigious French publisher Gallimard printed the dialogue in its journal,* Debat *(May-September 1989 issue).*

Historian Furet has summed up the French Revolution as "a magnificent event that turned out badly." It proclaimed the Declaration of the Rights of Man, seventeen articles setting forth the principles of liberty, security, freedom of speech, religion, and the press, the right to due process of law, and the right to change the government. It also deteriorated into a bloodbath that led to a dictatorship.

Cardinal Lustiger refused to let the celebration ignore the French Revolution's attacks upon religion and the clergy. He officially endorsed a campaign to canonize 181 priests and three bishops martyred by a French mob in 1792. "They preferred to die," he reminded his fellow Catholics, "rather than be unfaithful to the Pope and the Church."

In quintessential Lustiger fashion, he enlarged the scope of the dialogue to explore and explain the role of the Catholic Church in a democracy. These universal dimensions of the dialogue follow, without the parts that concentrated on issues that are specifically French.

---

*Translated by Jean-Denis Marzi, Ph.D.

The Church and Democratic Rights

Equality for all citizens is by its nature an abstraction because it encompasses individuals on different social levels and with different religious beliefs. In religious matters in France, the evolution of thinking has led to a softening of the rigid separation between Church and State by financial aid to private (i.e. Catholic) schools. But this evolution in no way touches upon public opinion in favor of maintaining separation of Church and State.

I agree completely. This evolution makes me hope that we are going toward truer democracy in France. . . . Let us compare the actual state of democracies. For example, American democracy. Though based on a separation of Church and State, which has its vigilant defenders, it is in general, much more tolerant toward a diversity of cults and opinions, including public expression of this diversity.

If the French Revolution did not explicitly wage war on the Catholic Church, it still held that conflict was difficult to avoid, given the Church's situation under the old order in France. The Church and the clergy were so involved in the old order and the monarchy that the fall of either in 1789 posed problems of temporal and spiritual confusion. To go back further to the end of the seventeenth century, when the Church brought about the persecution of Protestantism under Louis XIV and later of Jansenism, it had two costly victories. The consequences are visible in the eighteenth century with its spectacular secularization. We are touching here upon one of the most profound evolutions of our history. How do you view it?

Permit me to respond with two historical considerations which perhaps can be contested. The first interprets the relationship between political and religious power in the history of the French nation. The second goes beyond revolutionary events and poses more general problems about the relationship between revealed religions whose origins are in Israel and the pagan notion of state. The two considerations play off each other, but are of a different nature.

In the French Revolution, it was accidental that things went so wrong. But the conflict itself was not accidental, because it is found at similar times under similar circumstances.

Let me start with a given: unlike other European countries, France did not find its national matrix in Catholicism. In several countries, the Church came before the state and provided a certain consistency to the nation, either by language or culture. This is true of Spain and Poland. On the other hand, in France the idea of a nation does not coincide with the notion of Catholicism. . . . From this fact, there arose a subtle and sometimes violent game of enticement and rivalry between ecclesiastical power and the French monarchy which was succeeded by the republican state.

The state needed a certain sacredness to justify and legitimize its ambitions, and it found this justification in the Catholic Church. For their part, responsible members of the Church were too often tempted to make alliances with the governing power in order to establish a central place for Catholicism. They helped each other out, and from this stemmed battles and rejection. The government wanted to subjugate the Church, and the Church wanted the State to answer to it. The French retain a tormented memory of these rivalries, where the ambitions of the Church often provoked blood-thirsty intolerance and all-consuming greed devoid of scruples. This same conflict explains, in part, anticlericalism in France. . . . This is the first consideration I want to present.

A much more serious question takes shape against the backdrop of the French Revolution: the idea of a sovereign state. It is the question of whether there exists an "absolute" which would be incarnated and represented by the human institution of a state. Implicitly, the French Republican order answered: yes. For those who accept the unconditional revolutionary state, national sovereignty is absolute, which speaks of the right to ask anything of men, even their lives, because it declares that it is reasonable and just and promises to assure the happiness of its people. Therefore it is said to represent perfect virtue, right, and justice. Certainly, references are made to a Supreme Being, but ultimately national sovereignty is substituted for a living God, a quasi-idolatrous figure for the divine.

The sovereign state cannot tolerate that its citizens refer to anything else, whereas the religious conscience demands that one be free to call on God as the foundation and guarantor of all freedom. It is on this point that a fundamental conflict is based in terms of the biblical tradition on what is absolute. Does the state represent the absolute and can it therefore demand everything from all its citizens?

The answer is of capital importance. It covers the entire range of the rights of man. It is what gives meaning to the ideas of the Second Vatican Council and John Paul II: they see in religious freedom the foundation of all freedoms. The liberty of a moral and religious conscience is conceived as the freedom to worship on the same level as any other private activity. Religious freedom is defined by its content: it must be understood as an inalienable right, an absolute right for a human being to give the best of himself to Him whom we call God, Him who transcends man. It is therefore a freedom which is beyond the power of the state.

Even if the atheist does not believe, he must be given in his moral conscience rights that transcend the power of the state. The atheist's version might be that the state is not everything or the state is not absolute. Religious freedom, freedom of conscience, is not freedom to do whatever one wants to do. It is the inalienable right and the moral duty of each human being to turn himself freely toward what transcends all humanity. This freedom is the foundation for all the others. When the tyrant tries to overthrow it, everything is subverted and he wants to dominate everything.

Yet the Church remains more than reticent, even hostile to the evolution of democracy in another realm, that of morality. The dynamics of man reconstituting himself has led to permissive and hedonistic societies which the Church violently condemns.

Look closely at the social doctrine of the Church, the ensemble of its moral positions in economic and social matters, in terms of nonviolence, work, social organization, etc. One cannot speak of simply extending a helping hand toward modern society. The Christian position is not monolithic. It is not a scientific formula; it is not the last word on the varied aspects of social life. But it continues to contest, if need be, inequalities found in society as well as false utopias and misleading messiahs. It is modest in the face of grand systems—it does not pretend to substitute one ideology for another. But it intends to stay up-to-date and share the vision of society which it draws from Revelation and the idea of the dignity of man which comes from it. In social matters, therefore, there is a detachment from old structures and a recognition of political rules in a modern society with all their diversity and autonomy. The Church will not abandon a religious vision to a secular one.

In your comments, don't you misconstrue the difference between the natural rights of man rooted in divine will and the rights of man on a social level. The latter was the focus of the French Revolution. Two centuries later, isn't this the interpretation which dominates in our contemporary societies with their permissive morality, conditions which pose major problems to any religious vision of man and, above all, to the Catholic Church?

To place in opposition rights founded on the nature of man created by God — and therefore objective — to rights preoccupied with infatuation with the self is to rediscover humanism at its origins, as it prevailed in the sixteenth century. In the West, this is followed by a conflict between God and man, as if a victory for man could only happen at the price of "the death of God." It is as if the triumph of God presupposed the destruction of man, thereby carrying the problem to extremes. . . . In any case, it seems to me that the alternatives you describe are to be found even before Christian thought. But it does not seem to me that a drift toward a humanistic interpretation is sufficient to shed light on a Christian understanding of the rights of man.

One can attribute the universality of man to Christian origins. But aren't you faced with a glaring contradiction in terms of Christian thought? Instead of thinking of the rights of man as part of nature created by God, one sees them using the eyes of the French Revolution with society as product of the will of man.

161

In effect, there exists a disparity on this point, though we should not harp on it.

The American Declaration of Independence contains a capital point: the inalienable rights of man were given to him by God. There is also a reference to the Supreme Being in the French Declaration of the Rights of Man. However, the test is to know if the rights of man so presented can survive the test of time. I wonder if the experience of the last two centuries does not lead us to ponder the fragility of the base upon which our society rests. The body of these principles is based on conventions which have been more or less solemnly adopted by mutual participants. . . . Today we must ask ourselves if the rights of man, too often denied, do not need a firmer base than simple convention or a hypothetical and precarious social contract.

For my part, I think that ratifying the totality of human rights conforms to Christianity. But the question remains: how to find a universally acceptable and established base so that these rights can be effectively respected by public power. In the eighteenth century they would have said that the solution can be found in reason. I agree completely, and I am ready to commit myself to this proposition. But experience has demonstrated that reason has not been able to fend for itself, nor has it been able to make a forcible enough stand against power. The universality of reason is not understood once and for all at the moment it is proclaimed. One must verify and confirm it. And it seems to me that today the situation is urgent because reason is threatened from all sides.

The subjective definition of the rights of man encompasses a hedonistic drift. The sovereignty of the individual and that of public authority reenforce each other reciprocally in a consumer society. On one hand, one must give the one-dimensional individual his freedom while he is surrounded by ever-expanding material goods. On the other hand, one must give the "sovereign" what is needed for growth. These two values — the individual and sovereign authority — are limited by each other. For many people, their union seems to be absolute without admitting any other power or a transcendental reference. This mixture of individualism and social totalitarianism can only result in negation of the rights of man.

For modern society, it is difficult to recognize a basis for these rights that escapes the arbitrary nature of individuals. What prevents our society from becoming involved in the worst forms of excess? What prevents our society from committing the worst abuses under the name of democracy?

To clarify matters, let's take an example — the question of the right of abortion. The U.S. Supreme Court has recognized this as a matter of individual rights: in the case of women, the right to control their own bodies. This speaks to the crux of the matter. Here we have a perfect example of the subjective social element. What is striking is that after 200 years the United States and France — two democracies in which the rights of man regarding religion were spelled out differently — end up with the same interpretation of these rights, although it conflicts with that of the Christian churches.

Speaking of rights without a moral content is impossible. I am not taking the position from a religious perspective that the believer holds to a law and norm revealed to him by a divine will. Rather I speak of the hope of human consciousness to see the fundamental rights of man respected, to see the integrity of each person respected and protected by civil society, the state, and its institutions. Abortion poses more than legal problems. It is also a moral problem — whether abortion is compatible with respect for human life.

This is an insoluble philosophical dilemma and I don't pretend to solve even part of it. But I affirm that for an American judge in tune with the U.S. Supreme Court the right of women to decide the destiny of their bodies is perceived as being part of an individual's rights and freedoms.

It doesn't seem to me that French law allows such a right. If such a right materialized, we would have to examine in the light of reason the infinite consequence of such a principle declared to be legitimate. This would extend to many realms of legislation: the possibility of the right to euthanasia, the right to any sadistic practice (including irreversible mutation). And why not extract financial benefit? I cannot see how such a formulation so cursorily presented can be recognized as a universal right without constituting a decisive test for the future of Western democracies and modern culture.

In the U.S. Constitution, the Supreme Court is the ultimate decision maker in the interpretation not only of the law, but of the rights of man. Isn't the U.S. citizen bound by such a decision as a member of that system?

We are dealing with interpretations which are fallible and must be discussed openly in the name of reason and freedom of thought. I do not find that a decision by the Supreme Court stems from a scientific truth which instantly

requires my acceptance. I must respect the laws, but this civic obedience cannot supersede moral conscience. Moreover, to my knowledge, American legislation is less constraining than in France and it is even more strongly contested. Its resolution depends on the arguments advanced. Under these circumstances, it cannot impose a definitive dogma of the rights of man, especially when we are discussing an interpretation which can be contested.

The Supreme Court decision is but a decision of society, with all the uncertainty this entails. It is not dogma. It still leaves open the choice not to abort for women who do not wish to do so. This is compatible with pluralism and individual choice, whereas prohibition denies all this.

Except that it is the duty of all thinking free men — you will no doubt agree — to question constantly the morality of their actions. It is not enough for a law to be passed, even in keeping with democratic procedure, and then have no one question it. Is debate then totally closed?

Agreed, but let me point out that the interpretation of social thought, since it has been in a democratic setting, has been more and more individualistic and less and less in alignment with the traditional teaching of the Church. This movement is obvious and presents the problem of compatibility between the Church and modern democracy.

I am not sure that the hope inherent in the rights of man does not deny itself if it denies its origin. Human beings have rights because they have been created in the image of God.

But if we suppose that this process continues, aren't we faced with a fundamental question for the Catholic Church faced with the development of modern democracy?

I continue to believe that the problem is not that of the Church faced with democracy, but one of humanity faced with its own destiny. The hope of the Age of Enlightenment, as set forth at the beginning of modern society, now runs

the risk of falling into a blind and dangerous abyss. We have examples before our eyes of this perversion, notably the distortion of the hopes of socialism and Marx as seen in the actions of Lenin and Stalin.

How do you explain this irreversible phenomenon affecting our society and its morals?

Over a relatively short period of time, we have seen a drift in our morality. Is this irreversible? Let us consider the evolution of morals over a long period of time. Their reform — based on principles fundamental to the Decalogue and its spread by biblical and Christian tradition — always took centuries. There is a ferment at work unceasingly in the heart of society. Look at the opposition of Revelation to slavery and and suppression of slavery in the course of history.

On the other hand, observation of contemporary society confirms once again that humanity can lose its bearings by denying the source of its existence. Economic prosperity can certainly engender great injustice as much in the management of goods as in the management of human rights. I can, without sophism, manifest a respectful love for man,

founded on religious faith and on a personal dignity conferred by God. This can perhaps be a source of inspiration and a defense against a rationality which can lead man into hedonism and the decadence inherent in totalitarianism. Doesn't the hedonistic bent result — in the name of individuality — in the denial of another's individualism, such as the child who is going to be born? In the same

165

way, people have been penalized because of their class and their race. Fifty years ago, if I had been of the same ideology as my contemporaries, I would have been thrown into a crematorium.

We must completely reevaluate our idea of respect for life and the relationship of man to his body in our society. We no longer really have any idea of what the human body is. There is such technological power operating on man and his body that human beings are being mastered by technology and dehumanized. This is one of society's grave crises. Our time has not lost its reason, but its body, which has become just an abstraction as matter whose form can be arbitrarily chosen. By contrast, faith in the Church and redemption invites us to respect the human body and not to make it a machine or instrument, but to recognize it as a temple of the Holy Spirit.

To confront the issue on less theological grounds, it is certain that if we abandon the rights of man to the general consensus, we open the door to the monstrous aberrations of totalitarianism. A fundamental optimism leads us to constantly hope for a leap by humanity and for men who will always reinforce the truth of man. I place complete faith in this hope because I believe in the dignity of man and the divine source of this dignity. Believers receive as a gift of faith the duty to ensure that this fundamental dignity of man will never be forgotten.

Is this your understanding of the role of the Church in democracies?
The Church must always contest and put to discussion any attempt to destroy what is divine in man. In this realm, the continued reaction of the Catholic Church — although sometimes in the minority — plays a larger role than it appears.

One last question. It concerns the internal structure of the Church. It is a monarchical structure which was both mother and rival to European monarchies. How is this aspect of the Church compatible with the world of democratic citizenry?
Strictly speaking, I would not say the Church operates on a political model. Its makeup is original. It combines the personal character of decisions and responsibilities with the necessity for

consensus and union on the largest possible level. It has superimposed, autonomous allegiances and very indirect controls. We are, therefore, the opposite of a centralized monarchy.

The system of Church power has experienced various twists and turns over the course of time, but this always included debate leading to much consultation and resulting in turn in unity at all levels. Take, for example, the election of the Roman Pontiff. . . . It is the vote of the College of Cardinals which designates the new Pope. The Pope himself does not designate his successor. The distribution of authority and the makeup of the system of responsibility almost leads one to think of a feudal type of system. The Church, therefore, does not function like an absolute monarchy, even if power is concentrated in the hands of the Pope in certain areas. The fundamental principle is of a constant consensus unceasingly checking itself and the followers to whom it is responsible and must answer. It remains to say that this procedure — which calls for complete consent combined with authority — is not the image of modern democracy.

To return to our discussion, modern democracy is based on a purely subjective notion of the rights of man. The Church is tuned to objective rights based on the transcendence of God, which has revealed and expressed itself throughout history. No one can address this transcendence without obeying it and without the rules of discourse and exercise of power strictly measured by the Evangelist and the loving will of God.

This nonidentification of the Church with any political model is fundamental and inalienable, even though the daily life of the Church might be influenced by political models in any particular epoch. That is why the Church will not have any problems coexisting with modern democracies, since it didn't with royalty. The price that it will probably pay will be the same. It accepted a high price with the monarchy and will accept the high price imposed by other political systems.

Yes, but my question is a twofold one. It concerns what you just said about the relationship between the Church and temporal power. It also concerns another aspect: the internal pres-

sure in the Church from democracy, the opposition to hierarchy, the defiance of authority which is a dominant trait of democracy.

While the political education of Christians does affect the functioning of the church to which they belong, the functioning of the Catholic Church aims toward a communion. That involves a consensus which supposes alignments not along the normal line of authority, but through an act of faith greater than oneself.

At the same time, another type of relationship is established among the participants. The minority and majority cannot be conceived solely as conflicting forces where one comes out on the top of the other. It is like pieces of the truth which surpass a single piece and constitute a whole. Relationships based on political power are real, but they have nothing to do with faith and charity. Moreover, we do not only have an agreement of human wills alone. We have an agreement instituted through divine participation. It is the work and the gift of the living God.